You've got this.

This is the final stretch of your CPA Exam preparation – the Final Review. You've diligently studied these topics, and now it's crunch time. This Final Review has completely new content from the Becker CPA Exam Review and focuses on the key concepts on the CPA Exam. Remember, fortune favors the brave, but the CPA Exam favors the prepared.

Access Becker's Final Review

You will need to download the Final Review assets. To get started, log in to your account at **online.becker.com**, click the download icon and follow the download instructions.

What's inside

Your Final Review is designed to mimic the actual CPA Exam, and has all-new task-based simulations and multiple-choice questions. If you need help at any point, remember that you still have access to the features of the CPA Exam Review, including:

- SkillMaster videos that coach you through task-based simulations
- Access to 1-on-1 academic support from our experienced CPA instructors
- Unlimited practice tests to work on your weaknesses

You're not in it alone!

For tips, stories and advice, visit our blog at **becker.com/theplusside**. You can also collaborate with other Becker students studying REG on our Facebook study group at **facebook.com/groups/BeckerREGStudyGroup/**.

We want you to be prepared and confident when exam day rolls around. Here are some tips to keep in mind:

+ Arrive at least 30 minutes early on exam day.

+ Bring your NTS and two forms of identification.

+ Your cell phone is NOT allowed in the testing center, even during scheduled breaks.

+ No outside calculators are allowed. The testing software will have a built-in calculator for you to use.

+ Breathe. Relax. Ground yourself. You've got this.

Becker.

Join the community!

Becker.

This textbook contains information that was current at the time of printing. Your course software will be updated on a regular basis as the content that is tested on the CPA Exam evolves and as we improve our materials. Note the version reference below and select your replacement textbook under Replacement Products at **becker.com/cpa-replacement-products** to learn if a newer version of this book is available to be ordered.

CPA Exam Review

Regulation Final Review

For Exams Scheduled
After December 31, 2019

V 3.5

COURSE DEVELOPMENT TEAM

Timothy F. Gearty, CPA, MBA, JD, CGMA . . . . Editor in Chief, Financial/Regulation (Tax) National Editor

Angeline S. Brown, CPA, CGMA. . . . . Sr. Director, Product Management

Mike Brown, CPA, CMA, CGMA . . . . Director, Product Management

Valerie Funk Anderson, CPA . . . . Sr. Manager, Curriculum

Stephen Bergens, CPA. . . . . Manager, Accounting Curriculum

Cheryl Costello, CPA, CGMA . . . . Sr. Specialist, Curriculum

Tom Cox, CPA, CMA . . . . Financial (GASB & NFP) National Editor

Steven J. Levin, JD . . . . Regulation (Law) National Editor

Danita De Jane . . . . Director, Course Development

Joe Antonio . . . . Manager, Course Development

Shelly McCubbins, MBA. . . . . Project Manager, Course Development

CONTRIBUTING EDITORS

Teresa C. Anderson, CPA, CMA, MPA	Michelle Moshe, CPA, DipIFR
Katie Barnette, CPA	Peter Olinto, JD, CPA
Jim DeSimpelare, CPA, MBA	Sandra Owen, JD, MBA, CPA
Tara Z. Fisher, CPA	Michelle M. Pace, CPA
Melisa F. Galasso, CPA	Michael Potenza, CPA, JD
R. Thomas Godwin, CPA, CGMA	Jennifer J. Rivers, CPA
Holly Hawk, CPA, CGMA	Josh Rosenberg, MBA, CPA, CFA, CFP
Patrice W. Johnson, CPA	Jonathan R. Rubin, CPA, MBA
Julie D. McGinty, CPA	Michael Rybak, CPA, CFA
Sandra McGuire, CPA, MBA	Denise M. Stefano, CPA, CGMA, MBA
Stephanie Morris, CPA, MAcc	Elizabeth Lester Walsh, CPA, CITP

Permissions

Material from *Uniform CPA Examination Selected Questions and Unofficial Answers*, 1989–2019, copyright © by American Institute of Certified Public Accountants, Inc., is reprinted and/or adapted with permission.

Any knowing solicitation or disclosure of any questions or answers included on any CPA Examination is prohibited.

Regulation

Final Review Sections

Regulation Section I | *Ethics, Professional Responsibilities, and Federal Tax Procedures*

A Ethics and Responsibilities in Tax Practice

B Federal Tax Procedures

C Legal Duties and Responsibilities

Regulation Section II | *Business Law*

A Agency

B Contracts

C Debtor-Creditor Relationships

D Government Regulation of Business

E Business Structure

Regulation Section III | *Federal Taxation of Property Transactions*

A Acquisition and Disposition of Assets

B Cost Recovery

C Estate and Gift Taxation

Regulation Section IV | *Federal Taxation of Individuals*

A Filing Status and Dependents

B Gross Income

C Passive Activity Losses

D Adjustments and Deductions to Arrive at Taxable Income

E Tax Computations and Credits

F Alternative Minimum Tax

Regulation Section V | *Federal Taxation of Entities*

A Differences Between Book and Tax Income

B C Corporations

C S Corporations

D Partnerships

E Estates and Trusts

F Tax-Exempt Organizations

Introduction

Final Review is a condensed review that reinforces your understanding of the most heavily tested concepts on the CPA Exam. It is designed to help focus your study time during those final days between your Becker CPA Exam Review course and your exam date.

This Book

Becker's Final Review is arranged based on the AICPA's blueprints. The blueprints outline the technical content to be tested on each of the four parts of the CPA Exam. The blueprints can be found in the back sections of Becker's main CPA textbooks.

The Software

The Final Review software uses an interactive eBook (IEB) format. Watch the introduction video in the Final Review software for a tour of the IEB features.

We recommend progressing through this course in the following order:

- Review the IEB content, including the video introduction to each topic and the lecture audio associated with each page of the IEB.
- Work the embedded multiple-choice questions for each topic as you progress through the content.
- Work the related multiple-choice questions in the question bank for each topic. There are links from the IEB to the question bank.
- Once you have completed all of the IEB sections, topics, and multiple-choice questions, do the practice Simulations in the software.

Becker Customer and Academic Support

You can access Becker's Customer and Academic Support under Student Resources at:

http://www.becker.com/cpa-review.html

You can also access Academic Support by clicking on the Academic Support button in the Becker software. You can access customer service and technical support from Customer and Academic Support or by calling 1-877-CPA-EXAM (outside the U.S. +1-630-472-2213).

I

Ethics, Professional Responsibilities, and Federal Tax Procedures

1 Treasury Department Circular 230

The publication addresses the practice before the IRS of "practitioners" with regard to the rules governing the authority to practice before the IRS, the duties and restrictions relating to practice before the IRS, the sanctions for violation of the regulations, and the rules applicable to disciplinary proceedings. Ethical considerations address the responsibilities of the practitioner with respect to preparing returns and representing clients before the IRS.

1.1 Duties and Restrictions of the Tax Preparer

The tax preparer is responsible to the IRS and/or the client for the following:

- Refraining from willfully or recklessly signing a tax return or advising a client to take a tax position that the practitioner knows or should know lacks a reasonable basis or is a willful attempt to understate tax liability.

- Providing information requested unless the tax preparer believes in good faith and on reasonable grounds that the information is privileged.

- Avoiding delay of any matter before the IRS.

- Refraining from assisting anyone under disbarment or suspended from practice by the IRS.

- Adhering to the conflict of interest rules set forth by the IRS.

- Refraining from charging an unconscionable fee and only charge a contingent fee in certain allowable circumstances.

- Charging no more than the tax preparer's published written fee schedule, if one exists.

- Soliciting and advertising according to the parameters identified by the IRS.

- Adhering to "best practices" to provide clients with the highest quality representation.

- Refraining from endorsing or otherwise negotiating a client's refund check issued by the IRS.

- Refraining from notarizing a signature of any person in regard to any matter in which the tax preparer has an interest.

- Refraining from the unlicensed practice of law.

1.2 Standards With Respect to Tax Returns

1.2.1 Not Frivolous

A practitioner cannot advice a client to take a tax return position unless the position is not frivolous.

1.2.2 Reasonably Likely Penalties

The practitioner must inform the client of any penalties "reasonably likely" to apply with respect to a position taken on a tax return.

1.2.3 Practitioner's Reliance Upon Client-Furnished Information

Generally, a practitioner who signs the tax return or other document may rely "in good faith without verification" upon client-furnished information. The practitioner is not required to verify client-provided information; however, he must make reasonable inquiries if the client-furnished information appears to be questionable or incomplete.

1.2.4 Knowledge of Omission by a Client

The practitioner must advise the client promptly of any noncompliance, errors, or omissions in tax returns and other documents and the related consequences under the law.

1.2.5 Diligence as to Accuracy

The practitioner must exercise due diligence regarding (i) preparing returns and other documents; and (ii) determining the correctness of her/his representations to the IRS.

1.2.6 Return of Client Records

Generally, at the request of the client, the practitioner must return all client records.

1.3 Tax Advice

When a practitioner gives written advice regarding federal tax matters, the practitioner must base the advice on reasonable factual and legal assumptions, consider known relevant facts, use reasonable efforts to obtain relevant facts, not unreasonably rely on statements of the taxpayer or other persons, and refrain from taking into account that a return might not be audited.

1.4 Sanctions

The Secretary of the Treasury or her/his delegate, after conducting a proceeding, may censure (publicly reprimand), suspend, or disbar any practitioner from practice before the IRS if the practitioner (i) is shown to be incompetent or disreputable; (ii) fails to comply with Circular 230; or (iii) with intent to defraud, willingly and knowingly misleads or threatens a client or prospective client.

Treasury Department Circular 230 provides rules regarding due diligence with respect to certain types of written advice regarding tax matters. These rules apply to which of the following types of written advice?

1. Covered opinions, as defined in the provisions.
2. Excluded opinions, as defined in the provisions.
3. Written advice relating to an entity or plan that has been used for the principal purpose of tax avoidance.
4. All written advice concerning one or more federal tax matters.

2 IRC Code of 1986 (as Amended) and Regulations Related to Tax Return Preparers

Several sections of the Internal Revenue Code ("IRC"), and the related U.S. Treasury regulations promulgated there under, govern those individuals who prepare federal tax returns (income, estate, gift, etc.) for a fee. Civil liabilities and penalties may be imposed on those who are guilty of misconduct.

2.1 Conduct That Could Result in a Fine

- Preparing or signing a tax return when the practitioner does not have a valid tax preparer's ID;
- Understating a client's tax liability due to an unreasonable tax position;
- Understating a client's tax liability due to willful or reckless misconduct (negligent or intentional disregard of tax rules);
- Endorsing/negotiating a client's refund check;
- Failing to provide the client with a copy of his/her tax return;
- Failing to sign a tax return or refund claim;
- Failing to furnish the tax identification number of the tax return preparer;
- Failing to retain records properly;
- Failing to correct information returns;
- Failing to be diligent in determining a client's eligibility for the earned income credit;
- Aiding and abetting in the understatement of a client's tax liability; and
- Disclosing client supplied information without authority.

2.2 Preparer Responsibilities

A preparer must do the following:

1. Legally minimize the taxpayer's tax liability and abide by the tax code.

2. Make a reasonable attempt to obtain necessary information from the taxpayer and make inquiries if the information appears incorrect or incomplete. (Note, however, that the preparer is not responsible for verifying taxpayer-provided information.)

3. Recommend a tax return position only if the preparer has a good faith belief that position has a realistic possibility of being sustained if challenged.

4. Notify the taxpayer if the preparer becomes aware of a tax return error.

5. Upon becoming aware of a taxpayer's failure to file a return, inform the taxpayer on how to correct the situation.

6. Consider whether to continue a professional relationship if the taxpayer does not remedy the above situations (items 4 and 5); however, the preparer may not inform the IRS without the taxpayer's permission.

Question 2   MCQ-09712

A taxpayer presented her tax return preparer, Mr. Powell, with documentation supporting income she had earned as an independent contractor. Although Mr. Powell knew that the taxpayer's income should be reported on the taxpayer's Form 1040 (U.S. individual income tax return), he intentionally did not report the income on the taxpayer's tax return. Mr. Powell understated the taxpayer's liability because he believed keeping the tax liability low would help retain the taxpayer as a client. In this situation, Mr. Powell may be subject to which of the following penalties:

1. Understatement of taxpayer's liability due to failure to follow substantial authority by the tax return preparer.

2. Failure to file correct information returns by a tax return preparer.

3. Wrongful disclosure or use of tax return information by the tax return preparer.

4. Understatement of taxpayer's liability due to willful or reckless conduct of the tax return preparer.

---

1 The Internal Revenue Service Audit and Appeals Process

The federal income tax system of the United States is based on the self-assessment of taxes. All "persons" with taxable incomes exceeding certain amounts are required to file annual income tax returns and to remit taxes that are due in a timely manner.

1.1 Audit Process

The audit process is part of the enforcement system to ensure that this "voluntary" assessment and payment is actually occurring. A return may be examined (audited) for a variety of reasons, and the examination may take place in any one of several ways. After the audit, if there are any changes to the tax payable, the taxpayer either can agree with the changes and pay the additional tax or can disagree with the changes and appeal the decision. Interest on unpaid taxes may also be due.

1.2 Appeals Process

The Appeals Division is authorized to settle all tax disputes based on the hazards of litigation. Appeals within the IRS appeals process must come within the scope of the tax laws and cannot be on "moral, religious, political, constitutional, or similar grounds."

2 The Federal Judicial Process

When a taxpayer and the Internal Revenue Service cannot reach agreement on a tax matter using the administrative appeals process, the dispute must be settled in the Federal Court system. Either the IRS or the taxpayer can initiate the process. In the federal court system, the U.S. Tax Court, a U.S. District Court, and the U.S. Court of Federal Claims are considered trial courts. The U.S. Court of Appeals, the Federal Court of Appeals, and the U.S. Supreme Court are considered appellate courts (appellate courts do not hold trials). In most civil tax cases, the taxpayer has the burden of proof. In certain situations, however, the burden of proof shifts to the IRS.

Question 1 MCQ-09719

For a taxpayer who chooses to litigate a tax position, which of the following courts should the taxpayer choose to start in if he does not want to pay the disputed tax in advance?

1. U.S. Supreme Court
2. U.S. District Court
3. U.S. Tax Court
4. U.S. Court of Federal Claims

3 Penalties Imposed on Taxpayers

The Internal Revenue Code contains many sections setting forth penalties, both civil and criminal, which the Internal Revenue Service can seek to impose to the taxpayer.

3.1 Common Penalties That Apply to Taxpayers

- Earned income credit penalty
- Penalty for failure to make estimated income tax payments
- Failure-to-file penalty
- Failure-to-pay penalty
- Negligence penalty with respect to an understatement of tax
- Penalty for substantial underpayment of tax
- Penalty for substantial valuation misstatement
- Fraud penalties

3.2 Defenses Available to Taxpayers

Generally, a taxpayer can avoid any penalty by showing that the taxpayer had reasonable cause to support the tax return position, acted in good faith, and did not have willful neglect. In addition to this, various defenses (based on the standards of compliance) are available to taxpayers.

3.2.1 A Position That Is Not Frivolous

A frivolous position is a position taken on the return that is patently improper, and it is not a defense to avoid any penalty. A position that is not frivolous is not patently improper, but arguable. Not having a frivolous position is not a sufficient basis to avoid penalties—even if the tax return discloses the tax position.

3.2.2 Reasonable Basis Standard

The reasonable basis standard is a position that has at least a 20 percent chance of succeeding, one that is arguable but fairly unlikely to prevail in court. This standard is not met if the taxpayer fails to make a reasonable attempt to determine the correctness of a position that seems too good to be true. This basis will avoid the negligence penalty with respect to an understatement of tax that is not substantial and the penalty for rules or regulations, even if the taxpayer does not disclose the tax return position for which the taxpayer has a reasonable basis. This basis will avoid the substantial underpayment penalty only if the taxpayer discloses the tax return position (except for tax shelters) for which the taxpayer has a reasonable basis.

3.2.3 Substantial Authority Standard

The substantial authority standard is a position that has more than a one-in-three chance of succeeding but less than a more-than-50 percent chance of succeeding (the "more-likely-than-not" standard). This basis will avoid the substantial underpayment penalty even if the taxpayer does not disclose the tax return position (except for tax shelters) for which the taxpayer has substantial authority.

3.2.4 More-Likely-Than-Not Standard

The more-likely-than-not standard is a position that has more than a 50 percent chance of succeeding. With respect to certain nondisclosed tax shelters, this basis will avoid both the negligence penalty with respect to an understatement of tax that is not substantial and the substantial underpayment penalty.

Question 2	MCQ-09705

Irving R. Spayer has not filed federal income tax returns or paid any federal income taxes for the last several decades because he feels that the federal income tax is unconstitutional. Which of the following penalties might apply to him?

1. The failure-to-file penalty in the amount of 10% of the tax due for each year (or fraction thereof) the return is not filed.

2. The failure-to-pay penalty in the amount of one-half of one percent of the tax due for each month (or fraction thereof), up to a maximum of 25% of the unpaid tax.

3. The total of the failure-to-file penalty and the failure-to-pay penalty.

4. The failure to file penalty of $200 for each month or part thereof (up to a maximum of twelve months) the return is late.

1 Common Law Duties and Liability to Clients and Third Parties

1.1 Liability for Negligence

1.1.1 Liability to Clients for Negligence—Four Elements

- **Duty of Care:** The accountant must owe a duty of care to the party harmed.

- **Breach:** The accountant breaches by failing to use due care. Failure to use due care occurs when the accountant fails to act as a reasonably prudent accountant (usually a failure to follow GAAS or GAAP).

- **Damages:** There must be some type of harm suffered.

- **Causation:** The damages must be caused by the accountant's negligence.

1.1.2 Liability to Third Parties for Negligence—Privity Defense

- **Liability:** Accountants are usually not liable to third parties for negligence because there is no *privity of contract* (no direct relationship between the accountant and the third party). Privity is only a defense to a lawsuit for negligence. It is not a defense to fraud.

- **Exception:** An accountant is liable to third parties for negligence if the accountant had reason to know the third party would rely on the accountant's work. This is the *third-party beneficiary rule* or *intended user* rule.

- **Ultramares Rule (Minority View):** The accountant is liable to third parties for negligence only if there is privity of contract or the accountant knows the exact name of the third party who will be relying on the accountant's work.

1.2 Liability for Fraud

- **Actual Fraud:** Actual fraud has the same five elements covered in the section on contracts (**MAIDS**: **M**aterial misrepresentation of fact, **A**ctual reliance, **I**ntent to induce reliance, **D**amages, and **S**cienter).

- **Constructive Fraud or Gross Negligence:** Constructive fraud has the same elements of actual fraud, but scienter is replaced by a lower standard—reckless disregard for the truth.

Question 1   MCQ-09540

Rhodes Corp. desired to acquire the common stock of Harris Corp. and engaged Johnson & Co., CPAs, to audit the financial statements of Harris Corp. Johnson failed to discover a significant liability in performing the audit. In a common law action against Johnson, Rhodes at a minimum must prove:

1. Gross negligence on the part of Johnson.
2. Negligence on the part of Johnson.
3. Fraud on the part of Johnson.
4. Johnson knew that the liability existed.

Question 2   MCQ-09572

If a stockholder sues a CPA for common law fraud based on false statements audited by the CPA, which of the following, if present, would be the CPA's best defense?

1. The stockholder lacks privity to sue.
2. The false statements were immaterial.
3. The CPA did not financially benefit from the alleged fraud.
4. The contributory negligence of the client.

2 Confidential Client Information

Confidential client information generally cannot be revealed to others without the client's consent.

■ If subpoenaed, the accountant must testify, unless the given state recognizes accountant-client privilege.

■ Confidential information must be revealed to the state CPA society's voluntary quality control review board.

■ Working papers belong to the accountant, not the client, but the same rules of confidentiality apply.

Question 3   MCQ-09492

The accountant-client privilege:

1. May not be waived by the client.

2. Does not prohibit an accountant from disclosing confidential client information without the consent of the client to a voluntary quality control review board.

3. Is as widely recognized as the attorney-client privilege.

4. Only applies to written documents.

II Business Law

1 Formation and Termination

1.1 Formation

An agent is anyone authorized to act for another. Minors can be agents.

1.1.1 Requirements for an Agency

An agency requires an agreement, but does not require consideration or a writing. Only agencies for sale of land or agencies impossible to complete in one year require a writing in most states.

1.1.2 Power of Attorney

Power of attorney is a written authorization of agency.

- The principal, not the agent, is the only party required to sign the power of attorney.
- The agent need not be an attorney at law.
- A power of attorney usually limits the agent's authority to specific tasks.

1.2 Termination

1.2.1 Terminable at Will

Most agencies are terminable at will, but if either party breaches a contract by terminating it, he is liable for damages.

1.2.2 Termination by Law

The following terminate an agency immediately:

- Death or insanity of either party.
- Bankruptcy of the principal, but not bankruptcy of the agent.
- Failure of the agent to have a required license.
- Destruction of the subject matter of the agency.

1.2.3 Notice

If an agent resigns or is terminated by the principal, to terminate apparent authority, the principal must give actual notice to persons with whom the agent has dealt and constructive notice (e.g., by advertisement in the newspaper) to all others.

1.2.4 Agency Coupled With an Interest

Agency coupled with an interest is not terminable by the principal.

- An agent has interest in the subject matter of the agency (such as a security interest or a buyer of stock who was appointed the seller's agent to vote the stock).

- Death or insanity of the principal does not end this agency.

Question 1   MCQ-09559

Owner sells his stock in ABC Corporation to Buyer and appoints Buyer as his agent to vote the stock at a shareholders' meeting that will be held the following week. The agency appointment provides that it is irrevocable. Which of the following statements is true?

1. Owner can revoke the appointment anytime before the meeting despite the language stating that the agency is irrevocable.

2. Buyer's appointment will be revoked by operation of law if Owner dies before the shareholders' meeting.

3. The agency cannot be terminated by either Owner or Buyer because it is coupled with an interest.

4. The agency may be terminated only by Buyer.

---

2 Authority of Agents and Principals

2.1 Actual Authority

Actual authority may be either express or implied. Express authority is the power that the principal specifically tells the agent that the agent has. Implied authority is the power that the agent reasonably believes the agent has based on the communications and past dealings between the principal and agent (e.g., authority to do whatever is reasonably necessary to do assigned tasks; authority to do what the principal has allowed the agent to do in the past).

2.2 Apparent Authority

Apparent authority arises from the principal's communications or actions toward third parties, which make it appear to the third parties that the agent is authorized.

- The law looks to see if it was reasonable for the third party to believe the agent was authorized.

- Secret instructions given to the agent have no effect on apparent authority unless the third party was aware of the instruction.

Question 2

MCQ-09479

Terrence has been Pauline's agent in the liquor business for 10 years and has made numerous contracts on Pauline's behalf. Under which of the following situations could Terrence continue to have the power to bind Pauline?

1. Terrence lost his license to sell liquor in that state.
2. The death of Pauline without Terrence's knowledge.
3. The bankruptcy of Pauline with Terrence's knowledge.
4. The firing of Terrence by Pauline.

3 Duties and Liabilities of Agents and Principals

3.1 Duties of the Principal and Agent

- Unless otherwise agreed, the principal owes the agent the *duty to reimburse* the agent for expenses while acting on the principal's behalf, the *duty to compensate* the agent, and the *duty to indemnify* the agent for losses incurred while acting on the principal's behalf.

- Unless otherwise agreed, the agent owes the principal the *duty of due care*, the *duty to inform* the principal of all relevant facts, the *duty to account* for money spent or received, the fiduciary *duty of loyalty*, and the *duty of obedience*.

3.2 Liability for Contracts

3.2.1 Liability of the Principal

- The principal is liable for all authorized contracts made by the agent (whether authority was express, implied, or apparent and whether the principal was disclosed, partially disclosed, or undisclosed).

- The principal is not liable for unauthorized contracts unless the principal ratifies the contract.

3.2.2 Ratification

- The principal must know all relevant facts to ratify the contract.

- If the principal accepts the benefits of the contract knowing all of its material terms, the principal has impliedly ratified.

- In most states, the principal cannot ratify unless the agent indicated to the third party when making the contract that he was doing so on behalf of the principal.

- Once the principal ratifies the contract, the third party cannot withdraw from the contract.

3.2.3 Liability of the Agent

- The agent is liable (in warranty) for all unauthorized contracts.

- The agent is not liable for authorized contracts unless she was acting for an undisclosed or partially disclosed principal.

3.3 Undisclosed or Partially Disclosed Principal

- If the agent had authority, both the principal and the agent are liable in an undisclosed and partially disclosed principal case.

- The third party cannot withdraw from the contract because of an undisclosed or partially disclosed principal unless the nondisclosure was fraudulent.

3.3.1 Partially Disclosed Principal

The agent reveals to the third party that there is a principal, but does not disclose the principal's identity.

3.3.2 Undisclosed Principal

The agent never reveals to the third party that there is a principal involved. An agent for an undisclosed principal can only have actual authority, not apparent authority.

3.4 Liability for Torts—Respondeat Superior

- The principal is liable for all torts of employees committed while the employee was acting in the scope of employment (i.e., doing something in connection with the job).

- The principal generally is not liable for the torts of independent contractors.

- The difference between an employee and an independent contractor is that the principal controls the manner in which work is performed as to an employee but not as to an independent contractor.

- The principal is liable even if the employee disobeyed instructions.

- The agent is also liable for torts the agent commits, even if the agent was following the principal's orders.

Question 3

Able, on behalf of Pix Corp., entered into a contract with Sky Corp., by which Sky agreed to sell computer equipment to Pix. Able disclosed to Sky that she was acting on behalf of Pix. However, Able had exceeded her actual authority by entering into the contract with Sky.

If Pix wishes to ratify the contract with Sky, which of the following statements is correct?

1. Pix must notify Sky that Pix intends to ratify the contract.

2. Able must have acted reasonably and in Pix's best interest.

3. Able must be a general agent of Pix.

4. Pix must have knowledge of all material facts relating to the contract at the time it is ratified.

Question 4

Phil asks his employee Ed to take a company truck to deliver some lumber to a customer, Carl. After delivering the lumber, Ed drives 10 miles beyond the customer's house to visit his mother at her house. While pulling the truck into his mother's driveway, Ed negligently strikes a pedestrian, Vic. If Vic sues Phil for his injuries, will Vic likely recover?

1. Yes, because Ed was Phil's employee.

2. Yes, because Ed was driving Phil's truck.

3. No, because Ed was negligent.

4. No, because the collision did not occur within the scope of Ed's employment.

Notes

1 Formation

A contract is a promise or set of promises that the law will enforce.

1.1 Offer

1.1.1 Making an Offer

- An offer must be seriously intended, communicated, and definite in its terms.
- Advertisements and price quotes generally are not offers, but rather are invitations to deal.

1.1.2 Termination of Offers

- An offeror can revoke an offer. Revocation is effective when received. Most offers can be revoked any time prior to acceptance except option contracts, merchant's firm offers under the Sales Article, and offers for unilateral contracts where there has been a substantial beginning in performance.
- An offeree can terminate an offer through a rejection. The offeree can reject expressly (e.g., by saying "no") or through making a counteroffer, which is considered to be both a rejection of the original offer and an offer (of which the original offeror is now the offeree who may accept or reject). A rejection is effective when received.
- An offer can also be terminated by operation of law. For example, destruction of the subject matter, death or incompetency of either party, or illegality all would end an offer immediately.
- An offer will end at its stated time, and if no time is stated, it ends after a reasonable time.

1.2 Acceptances

An acceptance must be communicated, but it need not be in writing. An offer can only be accepted by the party to whom it was made; an offer is not assignable unless the offer is an option contract (i.e., consideration was given to keep the offer open).

1.2.1 Common Law vs. Sales Article

- At common law (e.g., contracts for land or services), an offeree must assent to every term in the offer without change or addition; otherwise the offeree makes a counteroffer (i.e., the mirror image rule).
- On the other hand, new or different terms in an acceptance of a contract under the Sales Article generally do not affect the validity of the acceptance and do not prevent formation of a contract.

1.2.2   Mailbox Rule

■ An acceptance is valid when sent if properly addressed and stamped and the offeree uses either the expressed means of communication or any reasonable means of communication if the means was not expressed.

■ If an offer states the acceptance must be received to be effective, then it must be received (i.e., one may opt-out of the mailbox rule this way).

1.3   Consideration

Consideration must have legal value and must be mutually bargained for.

1.3.1   Legal Value

■ Legal value is doing something you are legally free not to do or refraining from doing something that you are allowed to do. It need not have monetary value or be of value equal to what it is exchanged for.

■ There is no consideration given when you are already contractually obligated to perform. Past consideration is not valid consideration. Thus, to modify an existing common law contract, both parties must give additional consideration.

1.3.2   Mutually Bargained For

"Mutually bargained for" means consideration was given in exchange for the other party's consideration.

1.3.3   When Consideration Is Not Required

No consideration is needed to modify a contract under the UCC Sales Article, to make enforceable a promise to pay a debt barred by the statute of limitations, or where there is foreseeable and reasonable detrimental reliance.

1.4   Defenses to Formation

1.4.1   Fraud

Actual fraud has five elements—**MAIDS**:

M = **M**isrepresentation of **M**aterial fact or deliberate concealment (opinions do not count unless made by an expert).

A = **A**ctual and reasonable reliance: The victim actually and reasonably relied on the misrepresentation.

I = **I**ntent to induce reliance: The misrepresentation was made with the intention that it be relied upon.

D = **D**amages: The defrauder is liable to anyone suffering harm.

S = **S**cienter: An intent to deceive, done knowingly or intentionally.

1.4.2   Innocent Misrepresentation (Comparison)

Innocent misrepresentation involves the same elements as actual fraud, except there is no scienter requirement.

1.4.3 Fraud in the Execution and Fraud in the Inducement

- **Fraud in the Execution:** The victim never knew a contract was being made. It makes a contract void.

- **Fraud in the Inducement:** Occurs when the victim knows a contract is being made, but terms are misrepresented. This makes a contract *voidable* (the defrauded party can disaffirm or rescind).

1.4.4 Duress

Duress is forcing someone into a contract by threat of violence or criminal action. The duress must actually induce the victim to make the contract.

1.4.5 Mistake

- **General Rule:** A mutual mistake allows the adversely affected party to avoid the contract. A unilateral mistake usually is not a defense.

- **Exception:** *Unilateral mistakes of material fact* make a contract voidable if the other party *knew or should have known a mistake* was being made.

1.4.6 Illegality—Contract Generally Void

If the consideration or the subject matter of a contract is illegal or becomes illegal after the contract is made, the contract generally is *void* unless the illegality is merely because a party failed to have a license that is required for revenue-raising purposes.

1.4.7 Minority

- Minors can disaffirm *anytime* while a *minor* or within a *reasonable* time thereafter.

- Minors cannot disaffirm contracts for necessities.

- Minors can ratify only after becoming an adult. They must ratify the entire contract, not just part.

1.4.8 Incompetency and Intoxication

Legally incompetent persons are not bound by their contracts. Intoxicated persons can disaffirm only if they were incapable of understanding what they were doing when the contract was made.

Question 1   MCQ-09456

The president of Deal Corporation wrote to Boyd, offering to sell the Deal factory for $300,000. The offer was sent by Deal on June 5 and was received by Boyd on June 9. The offer stated it would remain open until December 20. The offer:

1. Constitutes an enforceable option.

2. May be revoked by Deal any time prior to Boyd's acceptance.

3. Is a firm offer under the UCC but will be irrevocable for only three months.

4. Is a firm offer under the UCC because it is in writing.

---

2 Performance

2.1 Statute of Limitations

Statutes of limitations provide that lawsuits must be commenced within a certain period of time (for contracts, four to six years is typical). Generally, if the statute of limitations period has expired on a contract, it is unenforceable. Actions for breach usually are measured from the time of the breach rather than from the time the contract was made.

2.2 Statute of Frauds

2.2.1 Contracts Requiring Some Type of Writing

Six types of contracts require some type of writing—**MYLEGS**:

M = **M**arriage: Contracts where *marriage is the consideration.*

Y = **Y**ear: Contracts *impossible to perform within one year.*

L = **L**and: Contracts involving an *interest in real estate.*

E = **E**xecutor: Contracts by an executor promising *to be personally liable* for the debt of an estate.

G = **G**oods: Contracts for the *sale of goods for $500 or more.*

S = **S**uretyship: Contracts to *act as a surety* (promise to pay the debt of another).

2.2.2 Type of Writing Needed to Satisfy the Statute of Frauds

- The "contract" itself need not be in writing; any type of writing that states the material terms is sufficient.
- The writing need only be signed by one party, but the contract can only be enforced against the one who signed.
- The terms can be stated in more than one document.

2.3 Parol Evidence Rule

- Prior oral or written statements and contemporaneous oral statements generally cannot be admitted into evidence at trial in an attempt to vary the terms of a fully integrated (i.e., seemingly complete) written contract.
- You may always introduce evidence of the following:
  - Subsequent modifications
  - Explanations of ambiguities
  - Fraud, duress, or mistake

Question 2 | MCQ-09520

Diel entered into a written contract to sell a building to Stone. The contract was properly recorded. Stone breached the contract and Diel has brought an action for breach of contract. Stone pleads the statute of limitations as a defense. Which of the following statements is correct?

1. The time period fixed by the statute is uniform throughout the states.
2. Recording of the contract stops the running of the statute of limitations.
3. The time period fixed by the statute of limitations begins when the contract is recorded.
4. The remedy sought by Diel will be barred when the period of time provided by the statute of limitations has expired.

3 Discharge and Remedies

3.1 Discharge

3.1.1 Discharge by Performance or Prevention of Performance

Performance or tender of performance discharges a party. If a party hinders another party's performance, the hindrance constitutes a waiver of the condition of performance.

3.1.2 A Material Breach by One Party Discharges or Releases the Other

■ **Exception:** At common law, if one party has substantially performed but commits a minor breach, no discharge occurs. The breaching party may recover under the contract, but damages are subtracted for the minor breach.

■ **Anticipatory Repudiation:** An anticipatory repudiation occurs when one party, prior to the time of performance, states they won't perform. The nonrepudiating party may cancel the contract, sue immediately, or wait until the time of performance and then sue.

3.1.3 Discharge by Agreement

■ **Accord and Satisfaction:** An accord is an agreement to substitute one contract for another, and satisfaction is the execution of the accord. Accord and satisfaction discharge the original duty. Until the accord is satisfied, a party may sue under the original contract or the accord.

■ **Novation:** In a novation, the parties agree to replace one party in a contract with a new party. It is the same deal, but with new parties. The creditor releases the old party and looks only to the new party for performance.

3.1.4 Discharge by Operation of Law

- **Impossibility of Performance:** Will release all parties to a contract. Examples of impossibility of performance are death of party in a personal service contract or destruction of the subject matter prior to performance.

3.2 Remedies

3.2.1 Compensatory Damages

An award of money to compensate for all foreseeable harm done.

3.2.2 Specific Performance

- Specific performance is a court order that the breaching party "specifically perform" contract duties. It is only used with unique property and never with personal service contracts.

- Courts will not award both money damages and specific performance.

3.2.3 Liquidated Damages

- The parties agree in advance what damages will be if there is a breach (e.g., forfeiture of a down payment).

- Liquidated damages must be a reasonable estimate of the actual harm likely to be caused by a breach, and not a penalty.

Question 3   MCQ-09612

Lark, CPA, entered into a signed contract with Bale Corp. to perform management advisory services for Bale. If Lark repudiates the contract prior to the date performance is to begin and Bale Corp. had not yet performed, which of the following is *not* correct?

1. Bale could successfully maintain an action for breach of contract prior to the date performance is due to begin.

2. Bale can obtain a judgment for the monetary damages it incurred as a result of the repudiation.

3. Bale could successfully maintain an action for breach of contract after the date performance was due to begin.

4. Bale can obtain a judgment ordering Lark to perform.

---

4 Sales Contracts

4.1 Formation of a Sales Contract

The Sales Article (UCC Article 2) governs sales of goods: moveable personal property. It doesn't govern contracts involving personal services, real estate, or intangible personal property.

4.1.1 Acceptance Need Not Mirror Offer

Under the Sales Article, an acceptance generally will be valid even if it includes terms different from or in addition to the terms stated in the offer.

4.1.2 Can Accept by Prompt Shipment

The seller can accept an order for goods by prompt shipment. If the seller ships nonconforming goods, the seller has both accepted and breached the contract, unless the seller notifies the buyer that the nonconforming goods were sent only as an accommodation.

4.1.3 Merchants

A merchant is one who ordinarily sells goods of the type being sold or who has special knowledge regarding the goods being sold or practices involved. Special rules apply to merchants.

4.1.4 Good Faith

All parties in a sales contract must act in good faith.

4.1.5 Can Modify a Sales Contract Without Additional Consideration

Contracts for the sale of goods can be modified without new consideration, as long as the modification is sought in good faith. To modify the price to $500 or more, a writing is required.

4.2 Merchant's Firm Offer Rule

- A merchant's firm offer is irrevocable without consideration.

- The offer must be for the sale of goods, made by a merchant, be in writing, and guarantee that it will be held open.

- The offer is irrevocable for the time stated, but the maximum period is three months. If no time is stated, it is irrevocable for a reasonable time.

4.3 Duties of Seller And Buyer

4.3.1 Seller's Basic Duties

- Unless otherwise agreed, the basic duties of a seller are to hold conforming goods for the buyer and give reasonable notice to enable the buyer to take delivery. If no place of delivery is stated, the place is the seller's place of business or, if none, the seller's home.

- The seller must make a perfect tender—no defects are allowed. If the goods are nonconforming in any way, the buyer may reject by notifying the seller within a reasonable time and following the seller's reasonable instructions.

- The buyer may reject all, some, or none of the goods.

4.3.2   Buyer's Basic Duties

Unless otherwise agreed, the buyer's basic duties are to accept conforming goods and pay for them at delivery.

4.4   Sales Statute of Frauds Exceptions

Generally, to be enforceable, contracts for the sale of goods for $500 or more must be evidenced by a writing signed by the party being sued (and include the quantity, unless it is an output or requirements contract). However, no writing is required with respect to: (i) specially manufactured goods or (ii) where a merchant sends another merchant a written confirmation of a contract that is sufficient to bind the sender and the recipient does not object within 10 days (confirmatory memo rule).

4.5   Rules for Risk of Loss (ROL)

Risk of loss (that is, whether the buyer or seller will bear a loss if the goods are damaged or destroyed) is determined by the delivery terms rather than by when title passes. However, title typically passes on delivery unless the parties agree otherwise.

4.5.1   Identification and Agreement

- For ROL and title to pass, the goods must first be identified as the ones that will fulfill the contract (set aside or designated as such).

- Once identified, the most important factor is the agreement between the parties.

- If the parties have not agreed, ROL is determined by the rules below.

4.5.2   Contracts Involving Transportation by Common Carrier

If transportation is by a common carrier, it is either a shipment contract or destination contract.

- **Shipment Contracts:** ROL and title pass to the buyer when the seller delivers the goods to a carrier.

- **Destination Contracts:** These are FOB contracts for a place other than the seller's location. ROL and title pass when goods reach the destination and the seller tenders delivery.

4.5.3   Contracts With No Common Carrier

- **Merchant Sellers:** ROL passes only when the buyer takes physical possession of the goods.

- **Nonmerchants:** ROL passes to the buyer upon the seller's tender of delivery.

4.5.4 Nonconforming Goods

ROL is always on the seller, regardless of the shipping terms.

4.5.5 Terms Affecting ROL

- **FOB:** "Free on board"; fixes the place where title and ROL will pass.
- **Sale on Approval:** ROL passes only after the buyer approves.
- **Sale or Return:** ROL passes on delivery, but the buyer has the right to return the goods.

4.6 Warranties—Express and Implied

4.6.1 Express Warranties

- Express warranties arise from a seller's statements of fact, description, sample, or model. The goods must conform to the statement of fact, description, sample, or model.
- The express warranty must have been part of the basis of the bargain.
- Once made, an express warranty generally cannot be disclaimed.

4.6.2 Three Types of Implied Warranties

Implied warranties require no written or oral words, and all implied warranties can be disclaimed.

- **Merchantability**

  Merchant sellers impliedly promise goods are fit and safe for normal uses. Such warranties may be disclaimed orally by an "as is" sale or by telling the buyer there is no warranty of merchantability. If a disclaimer is in writing, it must be conspicuous.

- **Title**

  All sellers impliedly promise good title and no unstated liens or attachments (encumbrances). Merchant sellers also promise no patent or trademark violations (infringements). To disclaim title requires very specific language (e.g., "as is," "with all faults," and the like are insufficient to disclaim the warranty of title). Can also be disclaimed by circumstances, such as a judicial sale where title is not guaranteed.

- **Fitness for a Particular Purpose**

  If the buyer tells the seller of a particular purpose for which the goods are needed and relies on the seller to provide goods fit for that purpose, and the seller knows of this reliance, there is a warranty that the goods will be fit for that purpose. Can be made by any seller—merchant or nonmerchant. Most disclaimers require a writing, except for an "as is" sale, which can be oral.

4.7   Remedies of Buyer and Seller

■ If one party has reasonable grounds to believe the other party will not perform when required, the unsure party may make written demand for assurances of performance. Failure to give assurance within a reasonable time is an anticipatory repudiation (below).

■ In the case of an anticipatory repudiation (that is, an indication by one of the parties that he or she will not perform), the nonbreaching party may: (i) sue immediately, (ii) cancel the contract, (iii) demand assurances, or (iv) await performance and sue later if the party does not perform.

■ Punitive damages are not available, and neither party may recover avoidable damages (that is, both parties have a duty to take reasonable steps to mitigate damages).

4.8   Remedies of the Buyer Upon Seller's Breach

■ Buyer is entitled to a perfect tender and may seek a remedy for any nonconformity.

■ The buyer can *rescind* (cancel) *and sue* for money damages.

■ The buyer can *cover* (buy suitable goods elsewhere) and charge the seller for the difference between the contract price and the cost of cover (or the difference between the market price and the contract price), plus incidental and consequential damages.

■ The buyer can *recover goods* from an insolvent seller if the goods are identified as the ones under the contract.

■ *Specific performance* is available if the goods are unique or the buyer otherwise cannot cover.

4.9   Remedies of the Seller Upon the Buyer's Breach—Unaccepted Goods

■ The seller can *stop delivery* for any breach.

■ If the buyer is insolvent the seller can *stop delivery and demand cash*.

■ The seller can *resell and sue for money damages*. The seller can get the full contract price if the goods cannot be resold or if the goods were destroyed after ROL passed to the buyer.

■ A *liquidated damage clause* is enforceable if it is reasonable and not a penalty.

4.10 Entrusting

If the owner of goods entrusts them to a merchant who deals in goods of the kind sold, and the merchant sells them in the ordinary course of business to a bona fide purchaser for value, the purchaser gets good title even though the merchant did not have good title.

Question 4

Greed Co. telephoned Stieb Co. and ordered 30 tables at $100 each. Greed agreed to pay 15% immediately and the balance within 30 days after receipt of the entire shipment. Greed forwarded a check for $450 and Stieb shipped 15 tables the next day, intending to ship the balance by the end of the week. Greed decided that the contract was a bad bargain and repudiated it. Stieb sued Greed. Which of the following will allow Stieb to enforce the contract in its entirety despite the statute of frauds?

1. Stieb shipped 15 tables.

2. Greed paid 15% down.

3. The contract is *not* within the requirements of the statute of frauds.

4. Greed admitted in court that it made the contract in question.

Question 5

Kirk Corp. sold Nix an Ajax freezer, Model 24, for $890. The contract required delivery to be made by June 23. On June 12, Kirk delivered an Ajax freezer, Model 52 to Nix. Nix immediately notified Kirk that the wrong freezer had been delivered and indicated that the delivery of a correct freezer would not be acceptable. Kirk wishes to deliver an Ajax freezer, Model 24, on June 23. Which of the following statements is correct?

1. Kirk may deliver the freezer on June 23 without further notice to Nix.

2. Kirk may deliver the freezer on June 23 if it first reasonably notifies Nix of its intent to do so.

3. Nix must accept the nonconforming freezer but may recover damages.

4. Nix always may reject the nonconforming freezer and refuse delivery of a conforming freezer on June 23.

Notes

1 Suretyship

1.1 The Relationship

1.1.1 Surety Defined

A surety is a third party who promises to pay a creditor if a debtor does not pay. The Statute of Frauds requires a writing signed by the surety for the surety's promise to be enforceable.

1.1.2 Gratuitous Surety

A gratuitous surety is not compensated for his or her promise to the creditor.

- Consideration is present if the gratuitous suretyship is created when the creditor-debtor relationship is created, because the consideration flowing to the debtor also serves as consideration for the surety's promise.

- A suretyship promise made *after* the creditor-debtor relationship has been created will not bind the gratuitous surety, due to lack of consideration.

- Any variation of the surety's risk by the creditor will release a gratuitous surety.

1.1.3 Compensated Surety

A compensated surety is paid for his or her promise to the creditor.

- A compensated surety's compensation serves as consideration for his or her promise, so the promise is binding even if made after the creditor-debtor relationship is created.

- Only a material variation of the compensated surety's risk by the creditor will release a compensated surety.

1.2 Creditors' Rights Upon Debtor Default

A creditor may do any of the following, in any order, upon the debtor's default. The creditor cannot be compelled by the surety to take any specific action.

- The creditor may immediately demand payment from the debtor.

- The creditor may immediately demand payment from the surety.

- The creditor may immediately go after collateral, if there is any.

- Exception: A surety who signs as a "guarantor of collectibility" promises to pay the creditor only after the creditor exhausts all remedies against the debtor. Additionally, the creditor must give notice of default to the guarantor.

1.3 Rights of a Surety

1.3.1 Subrogation

Once a surety pays the creditor in full, the surety acquires all of the creditors' rights (e.g., if the creditor was a secured creditor, the surety would have the rights of a secured creditor to the collateral).

1.3.2 Reimbursement (Also Called Indemnification)

The surety has the right to recover (i.e., to be reimbursed) from the debtor any money the surety had to pay the creditor due to the debtor's default.

1.3.3 Exoneration

Exoneration is the right of a surety to obtain a court order prior to default demanding that the debtor pay.

1.4 Cosureties and the Right of Contribution

1.4.1 Cosureties

Cosureties are two or more sureties of the same debt, even if unaware of each other.

1.4.2 Contribution

Once one cosurety pays the creditor, she may obtain a pro rata contribution from the other cosureties.

- The right of contribution is only available for cosureties.

- The proportional liability of each cosurety is determined by this formula:

$$\frac{\text{Amount guaranteed by individual cosurety}}{\text{Amount guaranteed by all cosureties}} \times \text{Amount paid} = \text{Amount owed by cosurety}$$

- If a cosurety's obligation is discharged in bankruptcy, the surety's agreed share should not be considered in determining the pro rata share of the remaining cosureties. The cosurety is eliminated from the calculation. Nothing can be collected from debts discharged in bankruptcy.

1.4.3 Defenses of a Surety Against a Creditor

- **Lack of a Writing and Lack of Consideration:** These are valid defenses for a surety.

- **Performance or Tender of Performance by Debtor:** This is a valid defense.

- **Fraud by the Creditor:** This is a valid defense.

  Fraud by the debtor to induce the surety to enter the relationship is not a valid defense for the surety against the creditor unless the creditor was aware of the fraud.

1.4.4 Personal Defenses of the Debtor

The surety may not use defenses that are personal to the debtor.

- Examples of personal defenses include bankruptcy of the debtor, the debtor's infancy or the debtor's insanity.
- The surety may use infancy, insanity, or bankruptcy as a defense if the surety was an infant, insane, or bankrupt.

1.4.5 Extension of Time

The creditor and debtor agree to extend the debtor's time of payment.

- Any extension of time discharges a gratuitous surety.
- A compensated surety is discharged only if the extension of time materially increased the surety's risk.
- If the creditor does not agree to extend time, but rather merely delays in collection, the surety is not discharged.

1.4.6 Release of Collateral by the Creditor

Release of collateral by the creditor discharges the surety to the extent of the monetary value of the collateral.

1.4.7 Release of a Cosurety

A release of a cosurety without the consent of the other cosureties releases the remaining cosureties by the amount of contribution they could have collected from the released cosurety.

Question 1   MCQ-09587

Which of the following rights may a surety not assert against his or her principal?

    1. Exoneration.

    2. Contribution.

    3. Subrogation.

    4. Reimbursement.

1.5 Creditors' Rights Outside of Suretyship

1.5.1 Creditors' Composition

A creditor's composition is an agreement between the debtor and at least two creditors that the debtor pays the creditors less than their full claims in full satisfaction of their claims. It results in the debtor being discharged in full for the debts owed the participating creditors.

1.5.2 Assignment for the Benefit of Creditors

In an assignment for the benefit of creditors, the debtor transfers some or all of his or her property to a trustee, who disposes of the property and uses the proceeds to satisfy the debtor's debts. The debtor is not discharged from unpaid debts by this procedure since creditors do not agree to any discharge.

1.5.3   Prejudgment Attachment

Before final judgment in a suit on a debt is rendered, if the creditor has reason to believe that the debtor will not pay, the creditor can ask the court to provisionally attach a piece of the debtor's property. The court then issues a writ of attachment (to the local sheriff) and the property is then seized so that if the creditor prevails, she will be assured of recovering on the judgment through sale of the property.

1.5.4   Judicial Lien

- If a debtor is adjudged to owe a creditor money and the judgment has gone unsatisfied, the creditor can request the court to impose a lien on specific property owned and possessed by the debtor.
- After the court imposes the lien, it will issue a writ (e.g., a writ of attachment), usually to the local sheriff, to seize property belonging to the debtor, sell it, and turn over the proceeds to the creditor.

1.5.5   Garnishment

Where a debtor is adjudged to owe a creditor money and the debtor has property in the hands of a third party (e.g., money the debtor is owed by his employer, money in a bank account, debts owed to the debtor), a writ of garnishment may be sought. The writ orders the person holding the property to turn it over to the creditor or be held personally liable for the value of the property not turned over.

1.5.6   Mechanic's Liens and Artisan's Liens

Under common law, a mechanic or artisan who works on property and either improves it or repairs it automatically has a lien on the property— for the price of the repairs—for as long as the property is in the lienor's possession. These liens are possessory—they dissolve as soon as the lienor lets the owner have the property back.

1.5.7   Materialman's Lien

Materialman's liens often are imposed in favor of contractors who perform work on, or provide supplies for, real property improvements. The unpaid materialman must file a notice with the local recorder of deeds in order to preserve his or her lien.

1.6   Fraudulent Conveyances

A fraudulent conveyance occurs when a debtor transfers property with the intent to hinder, delay, or defraud any of her creditors. A fraudulent conveyance is void or voidable and will be set aside in a proper proceeding.

1.7   Fair Debt Collection Practices Act (FDCPA)

The Federal Fair Debt Collection Practices Act (FDCPA) curbs abuses by collection agencies in collecting consumer debts. The act does not apply to a creditor attempting to collect its own debts; just to services that collect consumer debts for others.

1.7.1 Prohibited Acts

The act severely restricts collection agencies' ability to call third parties, such as relatives of the debtor, to indirectly pressure the debtor. A collection agency can contact third persons to discover a debtor's whereabouts, but may not disclose that it is a collection agency or that the debtor owes a debt.

2 Bankruptcy

2.1 Types of Bankruptcy

The types of bankruptcy tested are Chapter 7 (voluntary and involuntary); Chapter 13—individual debt adjustment; Chapter 11—reorganization (voluntary and involuntary); and Chapter 15—ancillary and cross-border cases.

2.1.1 Chapter 7—Liquidation

- The debtor's estate is liquidated and distributed to creditors.
- Most of the debtor's debts are discharged. The debtor gets a "fresh start."
- A trustee is appointed to handle the liquidation.

2.1.2 Chapter 13—Individual Debt Adjustment

- The debtor repays all or a portion of his debts over a three- to five-year period.
- A Chapter 13 trustee oversees the handling of the Chapter 13 proceeding.

2.1.3 Chapter 11—Reorganization

- Restructures the debtor's debts so the business can continue.
- No liquidation occurs and a trustee is not usually required.

2.1.4 Chapter 15—Ancillary and Cross-Border Cases

- Promotes uniform and coordinated legal regime for cross-border insolvency cases.
- A foreign representative may file for recognition of foreign proceeding or participate in a U.S. case.

2.2 Steps Required of Debtor Prior to Filing for Chapter 7 or Chapter 13

- For individual consumer debtors, mandatory credit counseling by an approved agency must occur no more than 180 days prior to filing.
- Current family monthly income is calculated by the debtor (average of six months preceding the filing).

- If the debtor's current family monthly income is equal to or less than the median income in her state, the debtor can file for Chapter 7 relief.

- If the debtor's income is greater than the median state income, the debtor must pass a "means test" to file for Chapter 7. Debtors failing the means test may have the case converted to Chapter 13 or have the case dismissed.

2.2.1 Means Test

The purpose of a means test is to see if the debtor has enough income to make payments under a Chapter 13 plan.

- The debtor calculates net monthly income (current monthly income minus certain allowed expenses).

- Allowed expenses include living expenses (e.g., food, clothing, transportation, etc.) in amounts set by the IRS, monthly payments for secured debts and debts receiving a priority in bankruptcy, payments for care of elderly or chronically ill household members, and certain expenses for elementary or secondary education.

- Net monthly income is multiplied by 60 to give a five-year total of disposable income. If this amount is $8,175 or less, the debtor can file for Chapter 7 relief.

- If the net monthly income is above $13,650, the debtor cannot file for Chapter 7, but may file for Chapter 13.

- If the net monthly income is between $8,175 and $13,650, the debtor must calculate if there are sufficient funds to pay 25 percent or more of the debtor's unsecured debts not entitled to a priority in bankruptcy. If there are insufficient funds to pay 25 percent of the unsecured claims, the debtor can file for Chapter 7. If there are sufficient funds, the debtor cannot file for Chapter 7, but may file for Chapter 13.

- A case may not be dismissed or converted to Chapter 13 if the debtor is a disabled veteran or if the debtor can show special circumstances (e.g., serious illness or a call to active military duty).

Note

Bankruptcy Code dollar amounts are adjusted for inflation every three years.

2.3 Specific Provisions of Chapter 7 Liquidations

2.3.1 Chapter 7 Voluntary

- The debtor voluntarily files for liquidation. A trustee is appointed to handle the liquidation.

- A debtor can file even if solvent, and spouses may file jointly.

- Debts will not be discharged under a Chapter 7 case until the debtor completes a government-approved financial management education program.

2.3.2 Chapter 7 Involuntary

- Creditors file to force liquidation. A trustee is appointed to handle the liquidation.

- With 12 or more creditors—three or more creditors must file who are owed $16,750 or more in aggregate in unsecured claims.

- With fewer than 12 creditors—one or more are required to file who are owed $16,750 or more in unsecured claims.

- If the debtor contests the involuntary proceeding, the order for relief is entered after a hearing has determined insolvency. The test for insolvency is not generally paying debts when due.
- Farmers and charities are exempt from Chapter 7 filings.

2.4   Specific Provisions of Chapter 11 Reorganizations

- The debtor submits a plan to restructure debts for the purpose of allowing the debtor's business to continue. The debtor has exclusive rights to submit the plan for 120 days. No liquidation occurs.
- The plan divides creditors into classes. Each class has an opportunity to accept the plan. The plan can be approved if as few as one class accepts the plan if a court finds it fair and equitable.
- Chapter 11 can be voluntary or involuntary. If involuntary, the same number of creditors and dollar requirements apply as with Chapter 7.
- A trustee is not usually required.
- Upon the court's final decree, the debtor pays off debts according to the plan.

2.5   Property Included in Debtor's Estate in Chapter 7 Liquidation

- The debtor's nonexempt property as of the filing date goes to the trustee to pay creditors. This includes proceeds of that property gained after the filing. Social Security and disability benefits are exempt. Certain things necessary to live (up to a certain amount) are also exempt.
- The debtor keeps most property acquired after the filing. Exceptions include property acquired within 180 days after the filing by divorce, inheritance, or insurance; this goes to the trustee to pay creditors.
- The trustee is free to accept or reject a lease.

2.6   Preferential Payments (Voidable Preferences)

Preferential payments are property transfers by the debtor before filing for bankruptcy that the trustee may set aside. The trustee may disaffirm voidable preferences if five tests are met.

1. **Transfer**

   The debtor must have transferred property to the creditor that benefited the creditor.

2. **Antecedent**

   The transfer must have been for an antecedent debt (an existing debt).

   - A new debt is not an antecedent debt (a contemporaneous exchange for new value).
   - Domestic support obligations (e.g., alimony, child support) are not counted as antecedent debts and cannot be disaffirmed.
   - Payments on secured debts (up to the value of the security) and current bills in the ordinary course of business are exempted.
   - Payments on consumer debts of up to $600 or less are exempted.

3. **Ninety Days**

- The transfer must have occurred within ninety days prior to the filing.
- The time limit may be up to one year prior to the filing if the creditor was an insider (e.g., relative of an individual debtor, officer of a corporate debtor).

4. **Insolvent**

The transfer was made while the debtor was insolvent (presumed during 90-day period before filing).

5. **More**

The creditor received more than he or she would have received in bankruptcy.

2.7 Priority of Debts in Chapter 7 Liquidation—11 Categories

Upon liquidation, debts are paid in the order of their priority. If there are insufficient funds to pay all debts within a given category, each debt within that category receives a pro rata share.

1st Secured creditors are paid up to the value of their collateral (category 11 for any deficiency).

2nd Domestic support obligations (alimony, child support, maintenance, etc.).

3rd Administrative costs of the bankruptcy proceedings.

4th Gap creditors (debts incurred after the filing, but before the order for relief is entered in an involuntary petition case).

5th Wages unpaid, but only if earned within 180 days of filing. The maximum priority is $13,650.

6th Employee benefits unpaid, but only if earned within 180 days of filing. The maximum priority is $13,650 per employee reduced by employee's wage claim.

7th Grain producers' and fishermen's claims against storage/processing facilities. The maximum priority is $6,725 per claimant.

8th Consumer deposits for goods and services paid for, but not received. The maximum priority is $3,025 per claimant.

9th Taxes unpaid, including federal state and local taxes.

10th Personal injury claims arising from intoxicated driving.

11th All other debts.

2.8 Discharge of Debtor in Chapter 7 Liquidation

Upon completion of a Chapter 7 proceeding, most of the debtor's debts are discharged. Only individuals can receive a discharge. Corporations and partnerships are dissolved.

2.8.1 Denial of Discharge

Certain actions by the debtor will preclude any discharge. Such actions include:

- Receiving a previous discharge within eight years of filing.
- Unjustifiably failing to keep adequate books and records.
- Fraudulent transfer or concealment of property within a year before or anytime after filing the petition.
- Refusal to explain a loss of assets.
- Committing a bankruptcy crime, such as making a false oath or claim, or giving or receiving a bribe.
- Refusal to obey court orders or to answer questions.

2.8.2 Debts Excepted From Discharge

Even if a discharge is granted, certain debts are not dischargeable (**WAFTED**). These include:

- Debts from causing **w**illful and malicious injury to others.
- Debts concerning **a**limony and child support.
- Debts resulting from **f**raud.
- **T**axes owed within three years of filing.
- **E**ducational loans.
- **D**ebts not reported by the debtor in the schedule of debts filed with the court and the creditor had no notice of the bankruptcy.

Question 2   MCQ-09560

Which of the following transfers made by the petitioner within 60 days of the filing of a bankruptcy petition can be set aside as a preference?

1. A $700 donation the petitioner made to his church.
2. A $700 current utility bill payment.
3. A $700 payment to a fully secured creditor to pay off the secured debt.
4. A $700 payment to the petitioner's brother to repay a loan the petitioner obtained six months ago.

Question 3   MCQ-09576

Which of the following is a reason to deny a debtor a discharge in bankruptcy?

1. Debtor owes debts arising from willful and malicious injury to others.
2. Debtor owes his home state and the federal government tax payments from the past two years.
3. Debtor received a discharge in bankruptcy five years ago.
4. Debtor owes debts arising from fraud.

---

3 Secured Transactions

3.1 Three Definitions

- **Secured Transaction:** Simply a debt that is secured by personal property (i.e., if the debt is not paid, the creditor has rights to take or sell the specified personal property–the collateral).

- **Purchase Money Security Interest Creditor:** A creditor who advances money or credit to enable a debtor to obtain property and retains a security interest in that property.

- **After-Acquired Property Clause:** A clause giving a creditor a security interest in the property acquired by a debtor after the security agreement is executed.

3.2 Three Requirements for Attachment

Attachment marks when a creditor's security interest is effective against the debtor. Attachment has three elements:

1. An agreement (written or oral) between the creditor and debtor. Written/electronic agreements must be signed/authenticated by the debtor and describe the collateral. Oral agreements are valid only if a creditor takes possession (i.e., a pledge).

2. The creditor must give value.

3. The debtor must have rights in the collateral.

All three elements must be met for attachment to occur.

Note

Filing is related to perfection, not attachment.

3.3 Ways to Perfect

Perfection sets the secured party's rights against third parties who also have an interest in the collateral. The following are different methods of perfection:

- The creditor can perfect by possession or control. This is the only way to perfect if the collateral is stocks, bonds, or negotiable instruments.

- The creditor can perfect by filing a financing statement that gives constructive notice to all third parties of the security interest. Filing must include the addresses of the parties, a general description of the collateral, and it must be signed or authorized by the debtor. This is the only way to perfect with intangible property, such as an account (receivable). The date of filing is used to determine priority even if the other steps needed for perfection are completed later.

- The creditor can perfect by attachment, an automatic but very limited type of perfection. Generally, this only occurs with a PMSI creditor in consumer goods and with small-scale assignments of accounts.

- There are also a few temporary periods of perfection (e.g., when the debtor moves to a new state).

3.4   Secured Creditor vs. Purchaser From the Debtor

- A creditor with a perfected security interest usually prevails over a purchaser of the collateral from the debtor.

- Exception: Anyone who buys from a merchant in the ordinary course of the merchant's business takes the property free of all security interests, even if he or she knew of the security interest, unless he or she also knew that the sale violated the security interest.

3.5   Priorities With Multiple Creditors

- With multiple creditors in the same collateral, the general rule is the first to file or to perfect has priority.

- Exception: A PMSI creditor in noninventory collateral (e.g., equipment) has priority if he or she files within 20 days of attachment.

- Exception: A PMSI creditor in inventory collateral has priority if he or she files prior to the debtor getting possession and gives written notice to creditors ahead of him prior to the debtor getting possession.

- If a debtor moves to a new state, collateral perfected in one state remains perfected for four months after the move.

3.6   Creditors' Rights Upon Debtor's Default

If a debtor defaults on a secured obligation, the creditor has three possible remedies:

3.6.1   Peacefully Repossess and Sell or Lease

- If the debtor defaults, the creditor can peacefully repossess (or have the sheriff repossess) and sell or lease (whatever is commercially reasonable) the collateral. The item may be sold at a public or private sale. The creditor must give proper notice to debtor and junior security interest holders prior to sale. The debtor can redeem prior to sale by paying all creditors in full.

- After the sale, the debtor is liable for any deficiency and is entitled to any surplus.

- A good faith purchaser for value at a sale takes free of the security interest and subordinate liens.

3.6.2   Keep the Collateral

- The creditor may peacefully repossess and keep the collateral after default, but must cancel the entire debt in consumer cases. The creditor must notify the debtor and other creditors in writing. If anyone objects, the creditor must sell the collateral.

- If the debtor has paid 60 percent or more of the price of consumer goods, the creditor must sell unless the debtor waives this right after defaulting.

3.6.3   Sue the Debtor for Debt

The creditor may forgo repossession and sue the debtor for the debt and reduce the claim to a judgment.

Question 4   MCQ-09615

Which of the following creditors would have priority in the same item of equipment collateral after the debtor defaults in paying all of the creditors?

1. A creditor who files a financing statement covering the collateral on January 2 and whose security interest attached and became perfected on January 20, when the debtor received possession of the collateral.

2. A creditor who perfected a security interest in the collateral by taking possession of it on January 25.

3. A lien creditor whose interest attached on January 28 when the sheriff levied on the equipment.

4. A creditor who loaned the debtor the money used to purchase the collateral and whose security interest attached on January 20 and was perfected by filing on January 30.

1 Securities Regulation

1.1 Definition of Securities and SEC Powers

The two main federal laws regulating securities are the Securities Act of 1933 and the Securities Exchange Act of 1934. State laws regulating securities are called blue sky laws.

1.1.1 Securities Defined

The term securities is broadly interpreted and includes almost any type of investment contract (generally, any investment in which the investor relies on management by others to make money).

- Examples: Stocks, bonds, debentures, warrants, stock options, collateral trust certificates and limited partnership interests.

- General partnership interests and certificates of deposit are not included.

1.1.2 SEC Powers

The SEC administers both acts. The SEC can suspend or revoke trading or registration for fraud or other illegality. The SEC can also conduct investigations and subpoena witnesses and records.

1.2 Liability Under the 1933 and 1934 Acts

1.2.1 Section 11 of the 1933 Act

Section 11 of the 1933 Act permits civil suits against issuers, directors, accountants, and attorneys. These are the same elements covered in the CPA legal liability section (acquired the stock, suffered a loss, and a material misrepresentation or omission of fact; no requirement of proving scienter, reliance, or negligence).

- Issuers are strictly liable for material misrepresentations.

- Accountants are liable unless they can prove due diligence.

1.2.2 Section 10b and Rule 10b-5 of the 1934 Act (Antifraud Provision)

Section 10b of the 1934 Act (the antifraud provision) permits civil suits against anyone buying or selling stock. These are the same elements covered in the CPA legal liability section (bought or sold the security, involvement of interstate commerce, suffered a loss, a material misrepresentation or material omission of fact, scienter and reliance, and suit must be brought within one year of discovery and three years of the violation).

1.3 Purpose of the 1933 Act and Registration Requirements

1.3.1 Purpose of the 1933 Act

- The purpose of the 1933 Act is to supply investors with sufficient information to make investment decisions.

- The SEC does not guarantee the accuracy of the information, does not give assurances against loss, and does not evaluate the financial merits of the offering.

1.3.2 Requirements of the 1933 Act

Two main requirements of the 1933 Act exist—to file a registration statement and to give a prospectus to investors.

- Only issuers, underwriters and dealers are required to register under the 1933 Act.

- The securities may not be sold until the *effective date* (20 days after filing).

- During the 20-day waiting period, the issuer cannot make written offers to sell, but may make oral offers. The issuer may also make limited written announcements. Examples of limited written announcements are the *preliminary prospectus* or "red herring" (it has essentially the same information as the final prospectus but conspicuously notes that it is not final) and *tombstone advertisements* (ads simply making known the future availability of the security).

- The registration statement contains a prospectus, audited financial statements, names of the issuer, directors, underwriters and 10-percent-or-more stockholders, and basic securities information, including the principal purposes for which the offering proceeds will be used.

1.4 1933 Act Exemptions From Registration

There are six main exemptions from registration:

- Intrastate offerings are exempt.
  - Rule 147—A transaction exemption available for offerings made within one state. Issuer must do 80 percent of its business in the state and be a resident of the state, purchasers cannot resell to nonresidents for six months, and general solicitation is prohibited.
  - Rule 147A—Like Rule 147 but solicitations can be made via the Internet and issuer need not be a resident of the state.

- Regulation D exempts private offerings under two rules: 504 and 506.
  - General solicitation is limited and purchasers cannot resell for one year.
  - Issuers are disqualified if affiliated with a covered person (insider such as issuer, director, or general partner) who is a bad actor (was convicted of or sanctioned for securities violations or fraud within past five years).
  - The SEC must be notified of issuance within 15 days after first sale.
  - Rule 504 allows issuances of up to $5 million within a 12-month period. There are no limitations on the number or type of investors. No specific disclosures are required. General advertising is prohibited unless the offering is registered with a state.

- Rule 506 provides an exemption for any amount to any number of accredited investors (institutions and rich people) and 35 or fewer unaccredited but financially sophisticated other investors. The issuer must ensure the unaccredited investors are buying for themselves. If only accredited investors purchase, no disclosure is required and general advertising is allowed. If there are any unaccredited investors, all must be given at least an annual report containing audited financials.

- Regulation Crowdfunding provides a transaction exemption for issuances made through the Internet.

  - Only issuers with less than $25 million in assets can use this, and the issuance is limited to no more than $1.07 million.

  - No investor may invest more than $107,000 within a 12-month period.

  - Only U.S. companies are eligible; companies registered under the 1934 act are ineligible.

  - Certain disclosures must be made (e.g., information about officers and major shareholders and financial condition of the company) which varies by the size of the company.

  - Resales are restricted for a year. And the bad actor disqualifications discussed above apply.

- **Regulation A:** Simplified registration is permitted for sales of securities of up to $20 million (tier 1) or $50 million (tier 2) in a 12-month period. General solicitation is permitted. Audited financials are required under Tier 2 but only reviewed financials are required under Tier 1. An offering circular or offering statement is given instead of a prospectus.

- **No Sale Transaction:** Issuer deals exclusively with existing stockholders without paying a commission.

- **Casual Sales by Ordinary Investors:** Only issuers, underwriters and dealers need register.

- **Exempted Securities:** Securities issued by banks, governments, common carriers, not-for-profit groups and short term commercial paper (nine months or less) are exempt from registration.

1.5   1934 Act Registration Requirements

- National stock exchanges, brokers, and dealers must register.

- The stock of reporting companies must be registered. A reporting company is an issuer with:

  - securities sold on any national stock exchange; or

  - 2,000 or more stockholders (or 500 or more stockholders who are unaccredited in any outstanding class) and with more than $10 million in assets.

1.6   1934 Act Reporting Requirements

1.6.1   Periodic Reports

Periodic reports are required for any issuer who must register stock under either the 1933 or 1934 Act.

- **10-K Annual Report**

  The annual report is filed with the SEC within 60 days (for large corporations, 90 days for small ones) of the end of the fiscal year. The 10-K contains audited financial statements.

- **10-Q Quarterly Report**

  The quarterly report is filed with the SEC within 40 days (for large corporations; 45 days for small ones) of the end of a quarter. The 10-Q contains unaudited financial statements.

- **8-K Current Reports**

  Current reports are filed with SEC within 4 days of a materially important event (e.g., new officers or auditors, changes in corporate control, etc.).

1.6.2   Reports Required Only by Reporting Companies (5 percent TIP)

- **5%** = 5 percent or more stockholders must file background information with the SEC and the issuer.
- **T** = Tender offers must be reported to the SEC by the one making the offer.
- **I** = Insider trading. All trading by officers, directors, 10 percent or more stockholders, accountants and attorneys must be reported to the SEC.
- **P** = Proxy statements and proxy solicitations must be reported to the SEC.

Question 1   MCQ-09542

A plaintiff wishes to recover damages from a securities issuer for losses resulting from material misstatements in a securities registration statement. In order to be successful, one of the elements the plaintiff must prove is that the:

1. Plaintiff was in privity of contract with the issuer or that the issuer knew of the plaintiff.
2. Plaintiff acquired the securities.
3. Issuer acted negligently.
4. Issuer acted fraudulently.

Question 2   MCQ-09574

Price Corp has only one outstanding class of stock. Price had previously issued 400,000 shares of this common stock. These shares are not traded on a national exchange. The original offering was exempt from registration under the Securities Act of 1933. Price has $10,500,000 in assets and 525 shareholders. All but five of the shareholders are unaccredited. With regard to the Securities Exchange Act of 1934, Price is:

1. Required to file a registration statement because it issued 300,000 shares of common stock.

2. Required to file a registration statement even though its shares are not traded on a national exchange.

3. Not required to file a registration statement because the original offering of its stock was exempt from registration.

4. Not required to file a registration statement unless insiders own at least 5 percent of its outstanding shares of stock.

1 Sole Proprietorship

1.1 Advantages

- One person owns and manages all affairs. The sole proprietor is free to transfer the business.

- It is easy to form and there is no need to file with the state.

- Unlike a corporation, the business is not taxed as a separate entity.

1.2 Disadvantages

- The sole proprietor is personally liable for debts of the business.

- A sole proprietorship ends with the death of the sole proprietor.

2 General Partnership

2.1 Formation of a Partnership

- A partnership is an association of two or more persons to carry on as *co-owners a business for profit*.

- A joint venture is similar, but involves an agreement to engage in a more limited undertaking. A joint venture is treated like a partnership in all respects.

- *No filing* is necessary for formation. The partnership is formed simply by the agreement of all partners to form a business; the agreement need not be "to form a partnership." The agreement can be oral unless the partners agree *in advance* that the partnership is to last for more than one year.

- Any partner breaching the agreement is liable to the partnership and to fellow partners.

- A partnership is a *legal entity* separate from its owners for most purposes *except for federal income tax* purposes and for obligations (partners are personally liable for the obligations of the partnership).

2.2 Liability of Partners

- All partners in a general partnership have *unlimited liability* for obligations of the partnership.

- They are jointly and severally liable for all partnership *torts* and for all partnership *debts*. If the partners vote to admit a new partner, the new partner is not liable for debts and obligations that existed before the new partner came to the partnership beyond any partnership contribution the new partner made.

2.3   Partners Are Agents of the Partnership and Agents of Each Other

- A partner can impose contract or tort liability on the partnership and fellow partners when acting with actual or apparent authority.

- An act of a partner apparently carrying on the business of the partnership in the ordinary course of business will bind the partnership through apparent authority.

- A partner has no apparent authority to make fundamental changes in the partnership, to admit liability in a lawsuit, or to submit a claim to arbitration.

- A partner owes the same duties all agents do (i.e., the duty of **d**ue care, the duty to **i**nform of all relevant facts, the duty to **a**ccount for money spent or received, the fiduciary duty of **l**oyalty, and the duty of **o**bedience [**DIAL-O**]).

- A partner acting without actual authority or breaching any duties is liable to other partners and the partnership.

2.4   Partners' Rights

- All partners have an *equal right to manage* unless otherwise agreed.

- Most decisions require only a majority vote.

- Exception: The following require *unanimous consent*:

  - Admitting new partners;

  - Transferring partnership property to others;

  - Admitting liability in a lawsuit or submitting a claim to arbitration; and

  - Making a fundamental change in the partnership (e.g., sell goodwill or change a written partnership agreement).

- Each partner has an *equal right to profits* unless otherwise agreed.

  - If division of profits is specified but not losses, then losses will *follow profits*.

  - Partners have no right to compensation unless otherwise agreed.

- Partners have the *right to be reimbursed* for loans made to the partnership and the *right to be indemnified* for liability incurred when properly acting on behalf of the partnership.

- All partners have the right to full information about the partnership (e.g., the right to inspect and copy books and records and the right to tax information).

2.5   Partnership Property

- Partners *own an interest in the business*; they *do not own partnership property*.

- Each partner has the right to use partnership property for partnership purposes, but not for other purposes.

- *Personal creditors of a partner cannot attach* partnership property.

- Partnership property is *not subject to a partner's liability for alimony*.
- If a partner dies, partnership property goes to the surviving partners, not to the deceased partner's heirs.

2.6   Assigning a Partnership Interest

- Any partner can assign or sell her/his/its partnership interest. Consent of fellow partners is not needed.
- The assignment does not dissolve the partnership. The assignor remains a partner and is still liable for all partnership debts.
- The only right the assignee receives is the right to the assignor's share of profits or surplus.
  - The assignee does not become a partner without the consent of all other partners.
  - The assignee is not liable for the assignor's share of losses.
  - The assignee has no right to participate in management, inspect books, etc.

2.7   Dissociation and Dissolution

2.7.1   Dissociation

Dissociation occurs when a partner ceases to be associated with the partnership business. It does not necessarily end the partnership business (it is just the term used to describe a partner's leaving the partnership).

- Dissociation may be voluntary (by the partner giving notice of withdrawal), or due to death, bankruptcy, expulsion, or some other event stated in the partnership agreement.
- The dissociated partner may be held liable for new debts of the partnership (for up to two years) as well, absent notice of the dissociation to third parties.
- Any partner has a right to withdraw from a partnership at will (one without a stated termination point) at any time.
- After dissociation, the dissociated partner's right to participate in management ceases, but the partner remains liable for partnership obligations and will continue to have apparent authority to bind the partnership until third parties are given notice of the dissociation.

2.7.2   Dissolution

Dissolution is the term that signifies that the partnership business is being terminated. Upon dissolution, partners must cease taking on new business and wind up the partnership's existing business. The following events cause a dissolution:

- The non-wrongful dissociation of a partner in a partnership at will.
- Bankruptcy of the partnership.
- In a partnership for a definite term or a particular undertaking, within 90 days after a partner's death or bankruptcy, a majority of the remaining partners vote to wind up the partnership.

2.8 Distribution Upon Dissolution

- Upon dissolution, creditors are paid first. This includes partners who are creditors.

- After creditors are paid, partners are credited or charged an amount equal to their capital contribution plus profits or minus losses. If this results in a partner having a negative balance, the partner will have to pay that amount into the partnership.

Question 1   MCQ-09103

Milton is a general partner in the Omni Company general partnership. Milton:

1. Has no apparent authority if the partnership agreement is contained in a formal and detailed signed writing.

2. Cannot be sued individually for a tort he has committed until the partnership has been sued and a judgment returned unsatisfied.

3. Can bind the partnership by renewing an existing lease that the remaining partners had decided to terminate.

4. Can bind the partnership by submitting a written admission of liability in a lawsuit brought against the partnership.

Question 2   MCQ-09143

Ted Fein, a partner in the ABC Partnership, wishes to withdraw from the partnership and sell his interest to Gold. All of the other partners in ABC have agreed to admit Gold as a partner and to hold Fein harmless for the past, present and future liabilities of ABC. A provision in the original partnership agreement states that the partnership will continue upon the death or withdrawal of one or more of the partners. The agreement to hold Fein harmless for all past, present and future liabilities of ABC will:

1. Prevent partnership creditors from holding Fein personally liable only as to those liabilities of ABC existing at the time of Fein's withdrawal.

2. Prevent partnership creditors from holding Fein personally liable for the past, present and future liabilities of ABC.

3. Not affect the rights of partnership creditors to hold Fein personally liable for those liabilities of ABC existing at the time of his withdrawal.

4. Permit Fein to recover from the other partners only amounts he has paid in excess of his proportionate share.

3 Limited Partnership

3.1 Formation of a Limited Partnership

■ A limited partnership is a partnership of two or more parties formed in compliance with a state statute for the purpose of providing limited liability for limited partners.

■ The certificate of limited partnership must be filed with the state.

■ There must be at least one general partner and one limited partner. A general partner may also be a limited partner in the same partnership at the same time.

3.2 Liability in a Limited Partnership

■ General partners have unlimited personal liability, as in a general partnership.

■ Limited partners have no liability beyond their promised or paid capital investment.

■ Under the Revised Uniform Limited Partnership Act of 1976 (but not under the Uniform Limited Partnership Act of 2001) limited partners have *very limited rights to manage or control*.

- A limited partner who manages is personally liable to all who thought he was a general partner.

- A limited partner whose name is used in the partnership is liable to all who thought he was a general partner.

■ Even under the 1976 Act, limited partners may vote on the following without incurring liability: voluntary dissolution of the limited partnership, fundamental changes in the business (including amendment of the certificate of limited partnership), and admission or removal of a general or limited partner.

3.3 Operation of a Limited Partnership

■ General partners have the same rights and powers as a partner in a general partnership.

■ Limited partners are just investors and, absent an agreement otherwise, have no right to manage or control beyond the voting provided for above.

■ Unless otherwise agreed, profits and losses are shared according to capital contributions, not equally.

■ Admission or removal of a general partner or limited partner requires unanimous consent of all of the general partners and all of the limited partners.

■ Limited and general partners may be secured or unsecured creditors of the limited partnership.

■ Both general and limited partners have the right to full information about the business, specifically including the right to inspect books and records.

- A limited partnership is dissolved upon the death, withdrawal or bankruptcy of a general partner. Changes in limited partners do not cause dissolution.
- General or limited partners may assign their limited partnership interest without the consent of others.
  - As in a general partnership, the assignee does not become a substituted general or limited partner.
  - The only right the assignee gets is the right to the assignor's share of profits.

Question 3   MCQ-09153

Unless otherwise provided in the limited partnership agreement, which of the following statements is correct?

1. A limited partnership can be formed with limited liability for all partners.
2. Upon the death of a limited partner, the partnership will be dissolved.
3. A person may own a limited partnership interest in the same partnership in which he is a general partner.
4. Upon assignment of a limited partnership interest, the assignee will become a substituted limited partner if the consent of two-thirds of all partners is obtained.

---

4 Limited Liability Partnership (LLP)

4.1 Definition

A limited liability partnership is similar to a partnership with two major differences, filing and liability.

4.2 Filing

An LLP must file a registration statement with the state. The statement must include the name of the LLP and a clear indication that the entity is an LLP.

4.3 Liability

- A general partner in an LLP is liable for his or her own negligence or wrongful acts and for the negligence and wrongful acts of anyone acting under the partner's direct control or supervision.
- A partner is not liable for the negligence of other partners or for those not under his or her direct control.
- LLP partners are also not personally liable for LLP contracts.

5 Limited Liability Company (LLC)

5.1 Formation of a Limited Liability Company

- The *articles of organization* of the LLC must be filed with the state. The *operating agreement* (the agreement between the LLC members) is not filed with the state.

- The articles of organization must contain the name of the LLC, the name and address of its registered agent, and the names of the persons who will be managing the company.

- Virtually every state permits an LLC composed of only a single member.

5.2 Liability in a Limited Liability Company

- LLC members have *no liability beyond their capital investment*, but are liable for any capital contribution not made.

- LLC members are liable for their own negligence.

5.3 Operation of a Limited Liability Company

- An LLC member may *assign his or her right to profits*.

  - The assignee does not become an LLC member without the consent of other LLC members.

  - The assignment does not dissolve the LLC.

- In most states, profits and losses are shared proportionally based on contributions, but under the Uniform Limited Liability Company Act (followed by only a few states but sometimes specifically tested on the exam), *profits and losses are shared equally*.

- Unless otherwise agreed, all LLC members have the *right to participate in management*. However, the articles of organization may provide that the LLC will be managed by managers selected by the members.

- Unless the LLC elects otherwise with the IRS, an LLC having two or more members is *taxed like a partnership* for federal income tax purposes.

- LLC members have the *right to full information* about the business, specifically including the right to inspect books and records.

- An LLC is dissolved upon the death, withdrawal, or bankruptcy of a member, unless the remaining members vote to continue the business.

Question 4   MCQ-09104

In general, which of the following statements is correct with respect to a limited liability company (LLC)?

    1. The operating agreement must be filed with the state.

    2. Unless otherwise agreed, an LLC is taxed like a corporation.

    3. An LLC must have at least two members.

    4. An LLC can be formed with limited liability for all members.

---

6 Corporation

6.1 Formation of a Corporation

6.1.1 Promoters

Promoters procure capital commitments and other agreements before the corporation is formed.

- They are liable for preincorporation contracts and remain liable unless a novation is executed.

- If the corporation accepts (or ratifies) the promoter's contract, the corporation is also liable.

6.1.2 Articles of Incorporation

The articles of incorporation must be filed by incorporators with the state. The articles must contain the corporation's name, the name and address of its registered agent, the name of its incorporators, and the number of shares authorized to be issued.

6.1.3 Bylaws

Bylaws govern the corporation's internal management and are not filed. The directors or incorporators usually adopt bylaws at the first business meeting.

6.2 Financing the Corporation—Financed by Debt Securities, Equity Securities, and Retained Earnings

6.2.1 Debt Securities

Debt securities are bonds and represent a debtor-creditor relationship. Unsecured bonds are called debentures.

6.2.2 Equity Shares

Equity shares evidence ownership of the corporation and are commonly called shares or stock. At least one class of common stock must have voting power.

6.2.3 Preferred Stock

Preferred stock has special rights over other stock, usually as to dividends and/or liquidation distributions.

- Preferred stockholders must be paid before any dividends are paid to common stockholders.

- Cumulative preferred stock has dividend carryovers to future years if the dividends are not paid in any given year.

6.3 Stockholders' Rights and Liabilities

- Stockholders have *no liability beyond their investment*.

- The corporate entity may be disregarded and stockholders held personally liable (called "piercing the corporate veil") if the corporation was formed to perpetrate fraud, if the corporation was undercapitalized at the time of formation, or if the shareholders commingle personal and corporate funds.

- Stockholders may inspect books and records at reasonable times unless the stockholders have an improper motive.

- The *preemptive right* is the right of a stockholder to buy newly issued stock being offered to the public in order to maintain his pre-issuance percentage ownership of the corporation. Preemptive rights are only available if the articles so provide.

- If, in bad faith, the directors refuse to vindicate or enforce rights of the corporation, stockholders may bring derivative suits to do so.

6.4 Stockholder Management Rights

- Stockholders have two main management rights: the right to elect (and remove) members of the board of directors and the right to vote on fundamental changes in the corporation.

- There are four main fundamental changes in the corporation that stockholders can vote on—**DAMS**:

    D = **D**issolution

    A = **A**mending the articles of incorporation

    M = **M**ergers, consolidations, and compulsory share exchanges

    S = **S**ale of substantially all the corporation's assets outside the ordinary course of business, but not buying all of the assets of another corporation

6.5 Stockholder Right of Appraisal or Dissenters' Rights

The right of appraisal (sometimes called dissenters' rights) is the right of the stockholder to be bought out by the corporation at fair market value after a corporation's fundamental change (i.e., **DAMS**) for which the stockholder did not vote to approve.

6.6 Approval Steps for Fundamental Changes to the Corporation

- The first step is passage of a resolution by a *majority* of the board of directors approving the change.

- Mergers (except short-form mergers) and consolidations must be approved by a majority of both boards of directors.

- The resolution is then submitted to the stockholders for approval.

  - They must receive a copy of the resolution and notice of the time, date, and place where the vote is to occur.

  - A *majority* of the stockholders must approve. Mergers and consolidations must be approved by a majority of the stockholders of both corporations.

- Articles (e.g., of merger, of amendment, etc.) must also be filed with the state.

6.7 Dividends

- Dividends are declared by the board of directors.

  - There is no inherent right of stockholders to receive dividends.

  - Directors are personally liable for wrongfully declaring dividends but have a defense of reasonable reliance.

- Once declared and communicated to stockholders, cash dividends are a debt and cannot be revoked. Once a dividend is declared, stockholders become unsecured creditors of the corporation.

- Stock dividends (i.e., dividends paid in the form of company stock instead of cash) do not reduce the assets of the corporation or increase a stockholder's percentage of ownership or wealth. Thus, they have no effect on earnings and profits for federal income tax purposes.

6.8 Directors and Officers

- The board of directors handles overall management and sets corporate policy; individually, directors have no power and are not agents of the corporation.

- Officers handle day-to-day affairs and are selected and removed by the board. Officers are agents of the corporation and owe the same duties all agents do (**DIAL-O**).

- The business judgment rule provides that directors and officers are not liable for their actions if they acted reasonably and in good faith.

  - Both officers and directors are liable if they were grossly negligent.

  - Directors may usually rely on reports of officers and other agents.

- Both officers and directors owe a fiduciary duty of loyalty to the corporation.

  - They must act solely in the best interest of the corporation.

  - They can have a conflict of interest in a transaction, and the transaction can be approved if fair to the corporation or the details are fully disclosed to the disinterested directors or shareholders, who then approve the transaction.

- Directors and officers generally may be indemnified by the corporation for losses in a lawsuit if they were acting in a corporate capacity.

Question 5   MCQ-09124

Trinket Corporation is being sued by its distributor, International, for nonpayment of debts. International will be able to hold Jasper Crumb, a shareholder of Trinket, personally liable for the company's debts if:

1. Trinket Corporation is overcapitalized.

2. The shareholder's personal assets are materially commingled with Trinket's assets.

3. Trinket's articles of incorporation allow for more than one class of stock.

4. Trinket has four shareholders, including Jasper Crumb.

III | Federal Taxation of Property Transactions

Notes

1 Capital Gains and Losses

Gains/losses on property held by the taxpayer (e.g., a personal vehicle, stocks and securities, real property not used in a trade or business, partnership interests, and other investment assets) are reported on Schedule D. The net gain or loss is calculated on Schedule D and reported as a single amount on Form 1040.

1.1 Gains and Losses From Dispositions

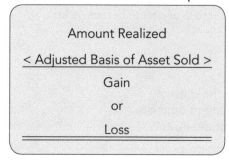

Amount Realized

< Adjusted Basis of Asset Sold >

Gain

or

Loss

- Amount realized includes cash, cancellation of debt, property at FMV, and any services rendered at FMV.

- Adjusted basis generally is the amount paid for the asset (cost) increased for any improvements and decreased for any depreciation (allowed or allowable).

- Gains/losses are long-term or short-term. Short-term gains and losses are for assets held for one year or less, and they are taxed using the same rates as ordinary income. Long-term gains and losses relate to assets held more than one year and are subject to a capital gains tax rate of 0, 15, or 20 percent depending on the taxpayer's taxable income. Although most taxpayers are subject to a 15 percent capital gains tax rate, a 0 percent capital gains tax rate applies to taxpayers with a low taxable income ($39,375 or less for single taxpayers in 2019) and 20 percent applies to taxpayers with a high taxable income ($434,550 or more for single taxpayers in 2019).

- Deduction of net long-term or short-term losses against ordinary income is limited to $3,000 ($1,500 if married filing separately). Excess losses are carried forward indefinitely.

1.2 Gift Property

Gifted assets are cash or property received as a gift. Generally, the gifted asset retains the donor's rollover cost basis at the date of gift. Gains and losses on the disposition of gift property are calculated as indicated above. However, if the property's FMV is lower than its basis on the gift date, the basis is determined by the ultimate sales price of the asset.

- If the sales price is higher than the rollover cost basis, the basis is the donor's basis, and the gain is equal to the difference between the sales price and rollover cost basis (minimizes gain).

- If the sales price is less than the lower fair market value, the basis is the lower FMV, and the loss is equal to the difference between the sales price and the lower fair market value (minimizes loss).

- If the sales price is between rollover cost basis and the lower fair market value, the basis equals the sales price, and no gain or loss is recognized.

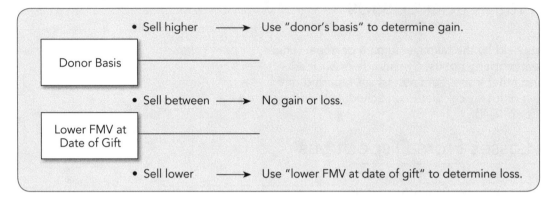

1.3 Inherited Property

- The basis of inherited property is generally the FMV at the date of death, unless the executor of the estate elects measurement on the alternate (lower) valuation date (six months after date of death).

- Inherited property is automatically classified as long-term property.

1.4 Gains/Losses Excluded, Deferred, or Disallowed

Certain gains and losses are excluded, deferred, or disallowed under the following circumstances.

1.4.1   Homeowner's Exclusion

Up to $500,000 (MFJ), or $250,000 (single, MFS or HOH) gain on personal residence sale is excluded from gross income.

For full exclusion, the taxpayer must have owned and used the property as the principal residence for two or more years during the five-year period ending on the date of the sale or exchange of the property. Either spouse can meet the ownership requirement, but both spouses must meet the use requirement (an exception exists for certain surviving spouses).

1.4.2   Involuntary Conversions

Gains realized on involuntary conversions of property (e.g., destruction, theft, or condemnation) are nontaxable to the extent that amounts are reinvested within two years (personal property) or three years (business property) after the close of the taxable year in which any part of the gain was realized.

The basis of the new asset is the same as the basis of the old asset, unless gain is recognized. If gain is recognized, the basis of the replacement property is its cost less the gain not recognized.

1.4.3   Divorce Property Settlements

Lump-sum payments and property settlements are nontaxable events. The recipient spouse's basis is the carryover basis, and there is no allowable alimony adjustment.

1.4.4   Exchange of Like-Kind Business Assets

Examples include exchanges of realty for realty. Nonrecognition of gain or loss exists when there is no boot involved. The basis of property received equals the basis of the property given up, decreased by any money received and increased by any gain recognized (due to boot received). Recognized gain is the lower of the realized gain or the boot received.

1.4.5   Installment Sale

An installment sale provides for deferral of the gain until the time when payments are received. When cash is received, gain is recognized in proportion to the gross profit percentage calculated on the original sale.

1.4.6   Treasury and Capital Stock Transactions

The issuing corporation does not recognize a gain or a loss on sales or repurchases of its own stock or on the reissuance of treasury stock.

1.5   Disallowed Losses

Certain losses are disallowed, meaning they are nondeductible.

1.5.1   Wash Sales

A loss is disallowed when a security is sold at a loss and is repurchased within 30 days before or after the sale date. Gains are taxed.

1.5.2   Related Party Losses

Losses resulting from related party sales (brother/sister, husband/wife, lineal descendants—not in-laws) are disallowed. Gains are taxed.

The purchasing relative's basis rules are the same as the gift tax rules.

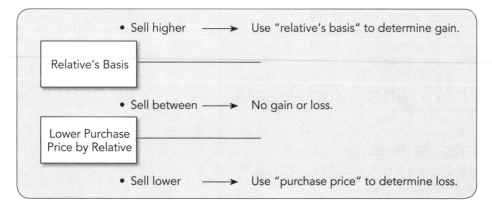

1.5.3   Personal Losses

Losses on disposal of nonbusiness assets (e.g., sale of a personal vehicle) are disallowed. Gains are taxed.

Question 1
MCQ-09566

On February 1 of the current year, Duffy learned that he was bequeathed 1,000 shares of common stock under his father's will. Duffy's father had paid $12,500 for the stock 20 years ago. Fair market value of the stock on February 1 of the current year, the date of his father's death, was $14,000 and had increased to $15,500 six months later. The executor of the estate elected the alternative valuation date for estate tax purposes. Duffy sold the stock for $14,500 on June 1 of the current year, the date that the executor distributed the stock to him. How much income should Duffy include in his current year individual income tax return for the inheritance of the 1,000 shares of stock which he received from his father's estate, assuming the estate tax law in effect for 2011 and forward?

1. $5,500
2. $4,000
3. $2,500
4. $0

Question 2
MCQ-09529

Conner purchased 300 shares of Zinco stock for $30,000 in Year 1. On May 23, Year 6, Conner sold all the stock to his daughter Alice for $20,000, its then fair market value. Conner realized no other gain or loss during Year 6. On July 26, Year 6, Alice sold the 300 shares of Zinco for $25,000.

What was Alice's recognized gain or loss on her sale?

1. $0
2. $5,000 long-term gain.
3. $5,000 short-term loss.
4. $5,000 long-term loss.

2 Section 1231, 1245, and 1250 Assets

2.1 Section 1231 Assets Defined

Section 1231 assets are depreciable personal and real property used in a taxpayer's trade or business for longer than one year.

2.2 Section 1231 Tax Treatment (Capital Gains/ Ordinary Losses)

2.2.1 Section 1231

Section 1231 provides for long-term capital gain treatment (when Section 1231 gains exceed Section 1231 losses) or ordinary loss treatment (when Section 1231 losses exceed Section 1231 gains) for sales or exchanges of Section 1231 assets. This treatment often allows for net Section 1231 gains to be taxed at lower rates (for individuals, estates, and trusts) and for net Section 1231 losses to be allowed as offsets to ordinary income.

2.2.2 Tax Issue

Use of MACRS depreciation typically accelerates the cost recovery over a period shorter than the economic life of the asset; therefore, when Section 1231 existed on its own, many Section 1231 assets were providing for ordinary losses for the depreciation on the asset and capital gains on the asset once it was disposed of. There was a significant unintended tax benefit that required a solution.

2.2.3 Tax Code Solution

Because of the issue mentioned above, Sections 1245 and 1250 were quickly introduced into the tax code. These sections removed some of the unintended tax benefits related to gains that existed when Section 1231 stood on its own. Net Section 1231 losses are still treated as ordinary losses.

Note

Recall that lower tax rates (0, 15, or 20 percent) often apply to net capital gains recognized by individuals, estates, and trusts. A net capital gain is the excess, if any, of net long-term capital gains over net short-term capital losses.

2.3 Section 1245—Applies to Gains on Personal Property (Section 1231 Assets)

2.3.1 Ordinary Income Portion

Upon disposal, Section 1245 requires recapture as ordinary income any gain up to the original purchase price (i.e., recapture 100 percent of the accumulated depreciation on the asset).

2.3.2 Capital Gain Portion

Excess gain (if any) is treated as a Section 1231 gain.

2.4 Section 1250—Applies to Gains on Real Property (Section 1231 Assets)

2.4.1 Assets Affected

Section 1250 applies only to real estate placed in service prior to 1987. Real estate placed in service after 1986 must use the straight-line depreciation rules of MACRS.

2.4.2   Ordinary Income Portion

Upon disposal, Section 1250 requires recapture as ordinary income the difference between the accumulated depreciation that would have been calculated under straight-line and what actually existed under the accelerated method used during the life of the property. (This is the recapture rule for individuals; the recapture rule for corporations is more complicated.)

2.4.3   Capital Gain Portion

Excess gain (if any) is taxed as capital gain at the lower capital gains rates.

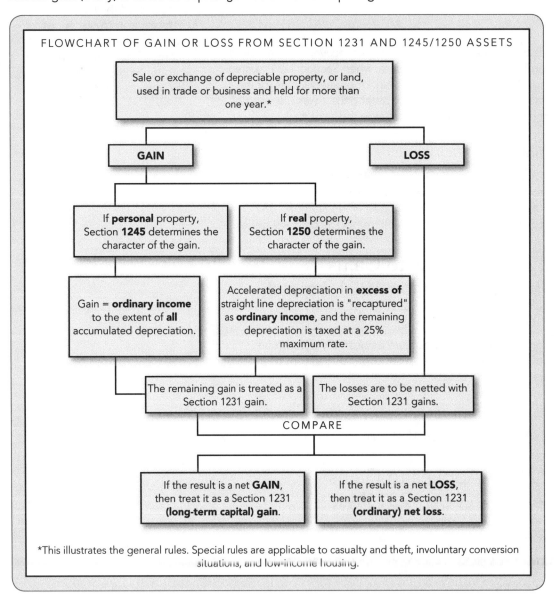

FLOWCHART OF GAIN OR LOSS FROM SECTION 1231 AND 1245/1250 ASSETS

Sale or exchange of depreciable property, or land, used in trade or business and held for more than one year.*

GAIN **LOSS**

If **personal** property, Section **1245** determines the character of the gain.

If **real** property, Section **1250** determines the character of the gain.

Gain = **ordinary income** to the extent of **all** accumulated depreciation.

Accelerated depreciation in **excess of** straight line depreciation is "recaptured" as **ordinary income**, and the remaining depreciation is taxed at a 25% maximum rate.

The remaining gain is treated as a Section 1231 gain.

The losses are to be netted with Section 1231 gains.

COMPARE

If the result is a net **GAIN**, then treat it as a Section 1231 **(long-term capital) gain**.

If the result is a net **LOSS**, then treat it as a Section 1231 **(ordinary) net loss**.

*This illustrates the general rules. Special rules are applicable to casualty and theft, involuntary conversion situations, and low-income housing.

Question 3

Bolton Company sold machinery for $45,000 on December 23, Year 7. The machinery had been acquired on April 1, Year 5 for $49,000 and its adjusted basis was $14,200. The §1231 gain, §1245 recapture gain, and §1231 loss from this transaction are:

	§1231 gain	*§1245 recapture gain*	*§1231 loss*
1.	$0	$45,000	$0
2.	$0	$49,000	$14,200
3.	$0	$30,800	$0
4.	$0	$34,800	$0

A Acquisition and Disposition of Assets

Task-Based Simulations

Task-Based Simulation: Capital Gains and Losses

Scroll down to complete all parts of this task.

Dennis and Kelly Green, ages 55 and 45, respectively, are married and file a joint income tax return. Information pertaining to the Greens' Year 9 (current year) stock transactions follows:

Purchased Stock Dispositions:

	Acquired	*Sold*	*Cost*	*Proceeds*
Walnut Company	6/30/Year 2	7/15/Year 9	$3,000	$6,500
XYZ Corp.	2/16/Year 9	9/22/Year 9	$5,000	$2,000

Inherited Stock Disposition:

In addition to the stock sales shown above, Kelly inherited 500 shares of ABC Corporation. Her father had purchased the stock at a cost of $5,000. The company is now bankrupt and out of business. At her father's death, April 1, Year 1, the FMV of the stock was $8,000 (alternate value was not elected). Legal documents related to the bankruptcy state that Kelly will receive nothing for her 500 shares.

In column B, enter the amount of the recognized gain or (loss) on the Greens' Year 9 Individual Income Tax Return. Enter gains as positive amounts and losses as negative amounts. If the response is zero, enter a zero (0). In column C, select the holding period from the option list provided.

		A	*B*	*C*
1			**Recognized Gain or (Loss)**	**Holding Period**
2	Walnut Company		123	▤
3	XYZ Corp.		123	▤
4	ABC Corporation		123	▤

In the box below, enter the net capital gain or loss that would be reported on the Greens' Year 9 individual income tax return.

[123]

Select an option below

○ Short-term

○ Long-term

| RESET | | CANCEL | ACCEPT |

Explanation

Row 2: $3,500 Gain | Long-term. Realized and recognized gain is $3,500. The $6,500 proceeds less $3,000 cost = $3,500. The stock has been held for more than a year; therefore, the holding period is long-term.

Row 3: ($3,000) Loss | Short-term. Realized and recognized loss is $3,000. The $2,000 proceeds less $5,000 cost = ($3,000). The stock has been held for less than a year; therefore, the holding period is short-term.

Row 4: ($8,000) Loss | Long-term. Realized and recognized loss is $8,000. The stock is worthless and no proceeds were received. This stock was inherited; therefore, the basis is the $8,000 FMV at date of death (alternative valuation was not elected). All inherited property is automatically long-term, regardless of how long the decedent had owned the property and regardless of how long the beneficiary owns the property.

Net Capital Gain (Loss): ($3,000) Loss. The one short-term item is a $3,000 loss. The two long-term items are a $3,500 gain and an $8,000 loss. These net to a long-term loss of $4,500. Together, the $3,000 short-term loss and the $4,500 long-term loss result in a total loss of $7,500. For individuals, the capital loss deduction is limited to $3,000 in excess of capital gains (note that corporations are not allowed a net capital loss deduction). Therefore, only $3,000 of the loss is deductible, and the remaining $4,500 loss is carried forward indefinitely. The tax law provides that short-term losses are deducted first. The entire $3,000 short-term loss is deducted in Year 9 and the $4,500 long-term capital loss is carried forward.

Cost Recovery

1 MACRS

The MACRS method is typically applied to depreciable assets placed in service after 1986. Questions on the CPA Exam generally focus on the half-year, mid-month, and mid-quarter conventions (this topic also applies to individual taxation, so questions covered in this topic will include some individual taxation depreciation questions).

1.1 Salvage Value

Salvage value is ignored for tax purposes (for MACRS).

1.2 Personal Property

- Generally, the half-year convention applies for MACRS depreciation (i.e., one-half year of depreciation is taken in the years of acquisition and disposal).
- The mid-quarter convention applies when more than 40 percent of depreciable property is placed in service in the fourth quarter of the year.
- Cost recovery (depreciation expense) is calculated using 200 percent double-declining balance for 3-, 5-, 7-, and 10-year property, switching to straight-line when advantageous.

1.3 Real Property

- Residential real property is depreciated using the straight-line method, mid-month convention over 27.5 years.
- Nonresidential real property is depreciated using the straight-line method, mid-month convention over 39 years.

1.4 Section 179 Expense Election

The taxpayer can elect to expense up to $1,000,000 in 2018 and $1,020,000 in 2019 of new or used property acquired during the year. The maximum deduction is reduced dollar for dollar by the amount of property placed in service during the taxable year that exceeds $2,500,000 in 2018 and $2,550,000 in 2019. These two amounts will be adjusted for inflation. The deduction is not allowed if a net loss exists or if the deduction would create a net loss.

B   Cost Recovery

Question 1   MCQ-09639

Michael Sima, a sole proprietor craftsman, purchased an amount of equipment in the current year that exceeded the maximum allowable Section 179 depreciation election limit by $20,000. Sima's total purchases of property placed in service in the current year did not exceed the limit imposed by Section 179. All of the property (including the equipment) was purchased in November of the current year, and Sima elected to depreciate the maximum amount of equipment under Section 179. Sima had bottom-line Schedule C income of $50,000 in the current year. Which method may Sima use to depreciate the remaining equipment in the current year?

1. Sima may not depreciate any additional equipment other than the Section 179 maximum in the current year and must carry forward the excess amount to use in the following taxable year.

2. MACRS half-year convention for personal property.

3. MACRS mid-quarter convention for personal property.

4. Straight-line, mid-month convention over 27.5 years for real property.

1 Estate Tax—Form 706

Estate Transfer Tax

Gross Estate
- FMV property
- Insurance proceeds
- Incomplete gifts
- Revocable transfers
- Income in respect of decedent

< Nondiscretionary Deductions >
- Medical expenses
- Administrative expenses
- Outstanding debts
- Claims against the estate
- Funeral expenses
- Indebtedness of property
- Certain taxes (e.g., taxes before death and state death taxes)

Adjusted Gross Estate

< Discretionary Deductions >
- Charitable bequests, unlimited
- Marital deduction, unlimited

Taxable Estate

Adjusted Taxable Gifts
- Post-1976 gifts that were taxed
- No double tax because subtracted later in this computation

Tentative Tax Base at Death

x Uniform Tax Rates

The "uniform tax rates" apply to both taxable gifts and estates.

Tentative Estate tax

< Gift Taxes Payable >
- Reduction by gift taxes payable on gifts made after 1976
- This eliminates double taxation of these gifts

Gross Estate Tax

< Applicable Credit >

Credit	
2019:	$4,505,800

This credit amount is equal to the tax, before credits, on an $11,400,000 tentative tax base at death.

Estate Tax Due

Fred and Amy Kehl, both U.S. citizens, are married. All of their real and personal property is owned by them as tenants by the entirety or as joint tenants with right of survivorship. The gross estate of the first spouse to die:

1. Includes 50% of the value of all property owned by the couple, regardless of which spouse furnished the original consideration.

2. Includes only the property that had been acquired with the funds of the deceased spouse.

3. Does not include any of the value of the property held as joint tenancy with right of survivorship (or tenancy by the entirety) because of the unlimited marital deduction.

4. Includes one third of the value of all real estate owned by the Kehls, as the dower right in the case of the wife or courtesy right in the case of the husband.

2 Gift Tax—Form 709

2.1 Annual, Inflation-Adjusted Exclusion

In determining the amount of gifts made in a calendar year, the donor may exclude the first $15,000 in 2018 and $15,000 in 2019 of gifts made to each donee. This annual exclusion is not available for a gift of a future interest (i.e., a gift that can only be enjoyed by the donee at some future date), even if the donee does receive a current ownership interest in the gift. A gift by either spouse may be treated as made one-half by each. This gift splitting creates an exclusion of $30,000 per donee in 2018 and $30,000 in 2019.

2.2 Unlimited Exclusion

- Payments made directly to an educational institution.
- Payments made directly to a health care provider for medical care.
- Charitable gifts.
- Marital deduction (must be a terminable interest).

2.3 Gifts—Present vs. Future Interest

2.3.1 Definition

The postponement of the right to use, possess, or enjoy the property distinguishes a future interest from a present interest.

▪ A present interest qualifies for the annual exclusion of $15,000, and in most instances would be removed from the estate.

▪ A future interest (or a present interest without ascertainable value) does not qualify for the annual exclusion and, unless the required time period has passed, will not be removed from the estate.

2.3.2 Future Interest Gifts

▪ Reversions (gifting assets and later getting the property back).

▪ Remainders (distributed at some future time).

▪ Trust income interests, where accumulation of income by a trustee is mandatory and accumulations are distributed at some future time at the discretion of the trustee.

2.3.3 Present Interest Gifts

▪ Outright gifts of cash or property.

▪ Trust income interests where annual or more frequent distribution is mandatory.

▪ Life estates (ownership of the right to use property presently but not ownership of the property itself).

▪ Estates for a term certain.

▪ Bonds or notes (even though interest is not payable until maturity).

▪ Unrestricted transfers of life insurance policies.

2.4 Gifts—Complete vs. Incomplete Gifts

Complete gifts qualify for the annual exclusion and in most cases are not considered part of the gross estate at death. However, incomplete gifts are included in the gross estate for purposes of computing the estate tax.

2.4.1 Complete Gifts—A Gift Is Considered Complete (and Is Subject to Gift Tax)

▪ Even though the donee is not yet born, provided his identity can later be ascertained.

▪ Despite the possibility that the property may revert to the donor at some future time.

2.4.2 Incomplete Gifts—Not Considered Complete (and *Not* Subject to Gift Tax)

■ **Conditional Gifts**

If a gift is subject to conditions precedent and will not be complete until the conditions have been met (e.g., a recipient will not get the gift unless he graduates from a four-year accredited college), the gift is incomplete.

■ **Revocable Gifts**

If the donor reserves the right to revoke the gift or change the beneficiaries, the gift is considered incomplete. The gift is complete when those rights terminate by reason other than the donor's death.

Question 2   MCQ-09502

Which of the following requires filing a gift tax return if the transfer exceeds the available annual gift tax exclusion?

1. Medical expenses paid directly to a physician on behalf of an individual unrelated to the donor.

2. Tuition paid directly to an accredited university on behalf of an individual unrelated to the donor.

3. Payments for college books, supplies, and dormitory fees on behalf of an individual unrelated to the donor.

4. Campaign expenses paid to a political organization.

Task-Based Simulations

Task-Based Simulation 1: Gift Types

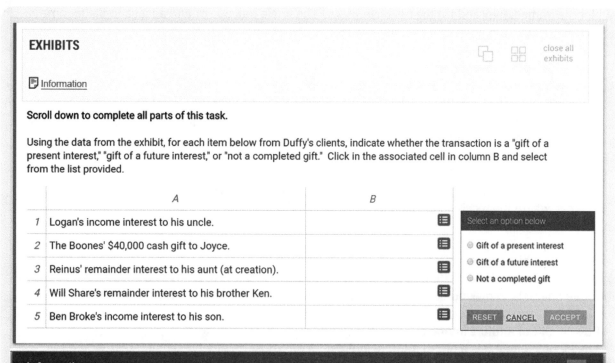

EXHIBITS   close all exhibits

📄 Information

Scroll down to complete all parts of this task.

Using the data from the exhibit, for each item below from Duffy's clients, indicate whether the transaction is a "gift of a present interest," "gift of a future interest," or "not a completed gift." Click in the associated cell in column B and select from the list provided.

	A	B	
1	Logan's income interest to his uncle.		▤
2	The Boones' $40,000 cash gift to Joyce.		▤
3	Reinus' remainder interest to his aunt (at creation).		▤
4	Will Share's remainder interest to his brother Ken.		▤
5	Ben Broke's income interest to his son.		▤

Select an option below
- ○ Gift of a present interest
- ○ Gift of a future interest
- ○ Not a completed gift

RESET   CANCEL   ACCEPT

Information   ☒

During the current year, various clients met with Duffy, CPA, for tax advice concerning the following situations and the possible gift tax liability on transfers they made:

- Logan created a $12,000,000 trust that provided his uncle with an income interest for five years, after which the remainder interest passes to Logan's brother. Logan retained the power to revoke the remainder interest at anytime. The income interest was valued at $5,000,000.
- Willard and Sharon Boone, U.S. citizens, were married for the entire current calendar year. Willard gave a $40,000 cash gift to his daughter, Joyce. The Boones made no other gifts to Joyce during the year. Willard and Sharon each signed a timely election stating that each made one half of the $40,000 gift.
- Reinus created a $4,000,000 trust that provided his father, Paul, with an income interest for his life and the remainder interest to go to his aunt, Mary, at the death of his father. Reinus expressly retained the power to revoke both the income interest and the remainder interest at any time.
- During the current year, Will Share transferred property worth $250,000 to a trust with the income to be paid to his 18-year-old niece, Mia Share. After Mia Share reaches the age of 25, the remainder interest is to be distributed to his brother, Ken Share. The income interest is valued at $120,000 and the remainder interest at $130,000.
- Ben Broke created a $400,000 trust that provided his son, I.M. Broke, with an income interest until he reaches the age of 30. When the trust was created, I.M. Broke was 18. The income distribution is to start when I.M. Broke is 21. After I.M. Broke reaches the age of 30, the remainder interest is to go to Ken's brother, Will B. Broke.

C Estate and Gift Taxation

Explanation

Row 1: Gift of a present interest
The income interest to Logan's uncle is a gift of a present interest since his uncle receives the income immediately and for the next five years. The uncle has use of and access to the income interest. Logan did not retain the power to revoke the income interest.

Row 2: Gift of a present interest
The cash gift to the Boones' daughter is an example of a gift of a present interest. A gift must be of a present interest, where the receiver has use of and access to the gift. Even though both Boones signed a timely election, the gift is greater than the $30,000 ($15,000 per individual) exclusion and will require a gift tax return for Willard and Sharon.

Row 3: Not a completed gift
The remainder interest at the trust's creation is not a completed gift. A gift must be of a present interest, where the receiver has use of and access to the gift. Reinus retained the power to revoke the remainder interest.

Row 4: Gift of a future interest
Since Will Share's brother, Ken, does not receive this gift until Mia reaches age 25, the gift is one of a future interest. In making this gift, Will Share did not retain any power to revoke the gift.

Row 5: Gift of a future interest
The income interest is a gift of a future interest. A gift must be of a present interest, where I.M. Broke has the use of and access to the gift. In this case, Ben Broke did not retain any power to revoke the income interest, so the income interest is a future gift.

Task-Based Simulation 2: Gross Estate

Scroll down to complete all parts of this task.

For each item below, indicate whether the transaction is "fully includable," "partially includable," or "not includable" in the gross estate by clicking in the associated cell and selecting from the list provided.

	A	B
1	Fair market value (FMV) of property owned exclusively by decedent.	☰
2	Life insurance proceeds (payable upon decedent's death) directed by decedent to be paid to his son (decedent had power to change beneficiary but had not exercised that power).	☰
3	Interest income earned by the decedent before his death and paid to his estate after his death.	☰
4	Gifts of cash distributed by the decedent to various friends and associates within the past three years. All gifts were below the annual exclusion amount.	☰
5	Marketable securities that have a higher fair market value (FMV) than their original cost basis.	☰

Select an option below

○ Fully includable in the gross estate

○ Partially includable in the gross estate

○ Not includable in the gross estate

RESET		CANCEL	ACCEPT

Explanation

Row 1: Fully includable in the gross estate

The gross estate includes the fair market value (FMV) at the date of death (or at an alternate valuation date, not to exceed six months after death) of all the decedent's property.

Row 2: Fully includable in the gross estate

The gross estate includes all property to which the decedent had incidents of ownership at death.

Row 3: Fully includable in the gross estate

All property entitled to be received, including income in respect of a decedent, is fully includable in the gross estate.

Row 4: Not includable in the gross estate

Gifts made within three years of the donor's death are generally not includable in the donor's gross estate.

Row 5: Fully includable in the gross estate

The gross estate includes the fair market value (FMV) at the date of death (or at an alternate valuation date) of all the decedent's property.

Task-Based Simulation 3: Research

A U.S. Estate Tax Return, Form 706, provides a minimum threshold for filing the return. What code section and subsection define the minimum amount of the credit allowed on an Estate Tax Return?

Enter your response in the answer fields below. Guidance on correctly structuring your response appears above and below the answer fields.

Type the section here.

Examples of correctly formatted sections are shown below.

IRC § [   ] ([   ])

ℹ️ Examples of correctly formatted IRC responses are IRC§1(a), IRC§56(a), IRC§54A(a), IRC§162(a), IRC§54AA(a), IRC§263a(a), IRC§1245(a), IRC§2032a(a), IRC§1400U-1(a).

Explanation

Source of answer for this question:

IRC Section 2010, Subsection (c)

Keywords: Unified credit estate tax

Notes

IV | Federal Taxation of Individuals

Filing Status and Dependents

1 Filing Status

Filing status is determined as of the end of the year (i.e., December 31).

1.1 Single

- This status applies to individuals who are single or legally separated and living apart.

- Any taxpayer who does not qualify for one of the other filing classes must use the single status by default.

1.2 Married Filing Jointly

- In order to file a joint return, the parties must be married at the end of the year, living together in a recognized common law marriage, or married and living apart (but not legally separated or divorced).

- This status is available even if one spouse dies during the year.

1.3 Qualifying Widow(er)/Surviving Spouse

- A qualifying widow(er), also known as a surviving spouse, may use the joint return tables and standard deduction for two years after a spouse's death, but he or she will not be able to use the personal exemption for the deceased spouse in those years.

- The taxpayer must maintain principal residence for a dependent child for the whole year.

1.4 Head of Household

- Must be not married, legally separated, or living apart from a spouse for the last six months of the tax year.

- Must not be a qualifying widow(er).

- Must not be a nonresident alien.

- Must maintain a household that for more than half the year is the principal residence of a "qualifying person": an unmarried son or daughter (not required to be a dependent, but must live with the taxpayer), father or mother (must be dependent but not required to live with the taxpayer), or other dependent relative (must live with the taxpayer).

Question 1

MCQ-09739

Bob provides more than half of his mother's support. His mother earns $6,000 per year as a hairdresser. She lives in an apartment across town. Bob is unmarried and has no children. What is Bob's most advantageous filing status?

1. Single
2. Head of household
3. Qualifying single
4. Supporting single

2 Dependents

Certain tax benefits, such as an advantageous filing status or certain tax credits, require either a qualifying child or qualifying relative. Each category has requirements.

2.1   Dependency Definitions

Dependency requirements are as follows:

Qualifying Child	Qualifying Relative
Close Relative: Son, daughter, stepchild, brother, sister, stepbrother/sister, or a descendant of these. Also includes adopted and foster children.	**S**upport: Taxpayer must provide > 50%. To claim exemption in multiple support situations, one must provide > 10%.
Age Limit: In general, child must be < 19 (or 24 if a full-time student) and younger than the taxpayer.	**U**nder specific amount of (taxable) gross income. This amount is $4,200 for 2019.
Residency: Same principal abode for > ½ tax year. If a foster child, must be for the whole year.	**P**recludes dependent filing a joint tax return.
Eliminate Gross Income Test: Does not apply.	**O**nly U.S. citizens or residents of U.S., Canada, or Mexico.
Support Test: Qualifying child may not contribute more than one-half of their own support.	**R**elative or **T**axpayer lives with individual for whole year.

Question 2

Jeff and Rhonda are married and have two children, Max and Jen. Max is 20, attends college in the Los Angeles area full-time and works as a stunt double for a television show while he is in school. Max earns $15,000 per year as a stunt double and lives at home when school is not in session. Jeff and Rhonda pay for Max's tuition and all his living expenses. Jen, who lives at home, is 18 years old and makes $18,000 per year working as full-time as an office administrator. Jeff and Rhonda pay for 65 percent of Jen's living expenses. In addition, Rhonda's mother, Joanne (a widow), resides with the family, earns $3,000 per year in interest and dividends from her investments, and receives $9,000 per year in social security benefits. Jeff and Rhonda receive no rent from Joanne and provide all the support she needs for the year. All those mentioned are U.S. citizens. How many people qualify as dependents for Jeff and Rhonda's income tax return?

1. Two
2. Three
3. Four
4. Five

1 Inclusions and Exclusions

All income is taxable income unless specifically excluded by the Internal Revenue Code. If income is taxable, include it in income at the fair market value ($ or property) and use the asset's fair market value as the basis. Nontaxable items are excluded from income, and the basis is the asset's net book value (as held by the person giving the asset to the taxpayer).

General Rule			
Event		Income	Basis
1. Taxable	=	FMV	FMV
2. Nontaxable	=	N -0- N E	NBV

2 Characterization of Income

2.1 Wages

Cash or FMV of property received as compensation for services is included in income.

- Partially taxable fringe benefits include items like life insurance premiums. Cost of $50,000 coverage is excluded from income; cost of excess coverage is included.

- Nontaxable fringe benefits are excluded from income (e.g., any employer-paid portion of medical/health insurance premiums and up to $5,250 of educational expenses).

2.2 Interest (Schedule B)

- **Taxable Interest:** Interest on corporate and federal bonds (not qualified Series EE savings bonds), bank accounts, and late tax refund payments.

- **Tax-Exempt Interest:** State and local bonds and qualified Series EE savings bonds (qualified when acquired after 1989, the taxpayer is over age 24, and they are used for higher education expenses of the taxpayer, spouse, or dependents).

2.3   Dividends (Schedule B)

- Amounts received that represent a portion of a corporation's earnings and profits are taxable income. Property dividends are taxable income at the property's FMV.

- Amounts that do not represent a portion of a corporation's earnings and profits are first credited as a return of capital to the extent of the individual's basis in the stock. Any excess amounts are then taxable as a capital gain.

- Dividends on stock held more than 60 days in the 120-day period beginning 60 days before the ex-dividend date are subject to a 15 percent tax rate for most taxpayers (0 percent for taxpayers with low taxable income and 20 percent for taxpayers with high taxable income).

2.4   State and Local Tax Refunds

State and local tax refunds are taxable if the taxpayer received a benefit for the itemized deduction of those taxes on a prior return (called the "tax benefit rule").

2.5   Alimony

Alimony received from a divorce or separation agreement executed on or before 12/31/18 is taxable income to the recipient and an adjustment from gross income for the payor.

- Payments must be in cash, be required by divorce decree, and be made "periodically" (e.g., monthly). Lump-sum property settlements are not alimony.

- Child support is *not* alimony. Child support must be paid first. If total payments do not cover all child support and alimony, they are first applied to child support and then to alimony.

2.6   Business Income (Schedule C)

Self-employed individuals report all business income and expenses allocable to business activities on Schedule C. A single amount is then transferred from Schedule C and reported on the face of Form 1040.

2.6.1   Business Income

Business income includes cash or fair market value of property received as compensation.

2.6.2   Business Expenses

Business expenses include cost of goods sold, business licenses, salaries and commissions paid to others (not to sole proprietor), depreciation, business meals (deduction limited to 50 percent), rent, insurance, travel, supplies, etc.

2.6.3   Net Income

Net business income is subject to both income tax (via inclusion on Form 1040) and self-employment taxes (calculated on Schedule SE and reported on page 2 of Form 1040).

2.6.4 Net Loss

Net loss is deductible against other Form 1040 income. For tax years 2018 and after, a taxpayer may not deduct an excess business loss for the year. For 2019, an excess business loss is defined as over $510,000 for married filing jointly and $255,000 for other taxpayers. Any excess business loss is carried forward as a net operating loss. Net operating losses may be carried forward indefinitely.

2.7   Individual Retirement Account Distributions

Distributions from IRAs are generally taxable when received. Amounts cannot be withdrawn before age 59½ (except in certain situations) without penalty. Distributions must start by the age of 70½ for traditional IRAs—called required minimum distributions (RMDs).

2.7.1 Types of IRA Accounts

- **Deductible (Traditional) IRAs:** Contributions are deductible. Distributions are taxable as ordinary income when received.

- **Roth IRAs:** Contributions are nondeductible. Qualified distributions are nontaxable when received.

- **Nondeductible IRAs:** Contributions are nondeductible. Distributions of original contributions are nontaxable, but distribution of the earnings is taxable.

2.7.2 Penalty Tax (10 percent)

- **General Rule:** Applies to premature distributions (before required ages) in addition to the income tax on the distributions.

- **Exceptions:** The penalty tax does not apply if the distribution was used for a first-time home purchase ($10,000 max free of penalty tax if used within 120 days of the distribution), medical insurance (for the unemployed), medical expenses in excess of 10 percent of AGI, disability, education expenses, or death.

2.8   Miscellaneous Taxable Income Items

- Prizes and awards.

- For gambling and winnings, losses are deductible only to the extent of winnings.

- Unemployment compensation.

2.9   Partially Taxable Items of Income

- Social Security income (depending upon income levels).

- For scholarships and fellowships, amounts not used for qualified expenditures and those paid to a non-degree-seeking student are taxable. Graduate teaching assistant tuition reductions are taxable if it is the only form of compensation.

B Gross Income

2.10 Nontaxable Items

- Life insurance proceeds
- Gifts and inheritances
- Medicare benefits
- Workers' compensation
- Personal physical injury awards

Question 1   MCQ-09481

Kyle and Kaylie were divorced in February 2018. The divorce decree required that Kyle give Kaylie $20,000 in exchange for keeping the house they both owned. In addition, beginning in March Kyle is to pay Kaylie $3,000 per month under the divorce decree. Kyle and Kaylie have two children, Kevin and Kelly. Also beginning in March, Kyle is required to pay $2,000 per month for the support of Kevin and Kelly. During 2018, Kyle paid Kaylie a total of $45,000. How much is taxable to Kaylie for 2018?

1. $5,000
2. $20,000
3. $25,000
4. $45,000

Question 2   MCQ-09450

Jeffrey Dean, a Master's Degree candidate at North State Central University, was awarded a $15,000 scholarship from North State Central in the current year. During the current year, he paid the following expenses:

Tuition	$12,000
Books	1,000
Fees	500
Room & Board	1,500

In addition, he received $6,000 for teaching two undergraduate accounting courses. What amount must be included in Dean's gross income?

1. $0
2. $6,000
3. $7,500
4. $21,000

3 Employee Stock Options

3.1 Nonqualified Options

3.1.1 Employee Taxation

A nonqualified option is generally taxed when granted if the option has a readily ascertainable value. Otherwise, the option is taxed when exercised.

3.1.2 Employer Taxation

Generally, an employer may deduct the value of the stock option as a business expense in the same year that the employee is required to recognize the option as ordinary income.

3.2 Incentive Stock Options (ISO) and Employee Stock Purchase Plans (ESPP)

ISOs and ESPPs are types of qualified options. An ISO is a right to purchase the stock at a discount. An ESPP allows employees to purchase stock at a discount.

3.2.1 Employee Taxation

If certain conditions are met, there is no taxation when ISOs and ESPPs are granted or exercised. A gain or loss is recognized on the subsequent sale of the stock.

3.2.2 Employer Taxation

Generally, an employer does not receive a tax deduction for an ISO or an ESPP because it is not considered compensation income to the employee.

B Gross Income

Task-Based Simulations

Task-Based Simulation 1: Interest and Dividend Income

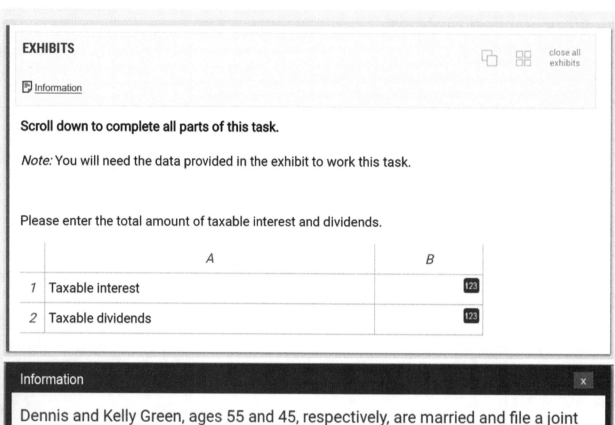

EXHIBITS   close all exhibits

Information

Scroll down to complete all parts of this task.

Note: You will need the data provided in the exhibit to work this task.

Please enter the total amount of taxable interest and dividends.

	A	B
1	Taxable interest	123
2	Taxable dividends	123

Information   x

Dennis and Kelly Green, ages 55 and 45, respectively, are married and file a joint income tax return. Their current year interest and dividend income follows:

Interest

Greenpoint Bank	$ 1,300
Whitewater Savings & Loan	1,000
Interest from Washington County bonds	500
Bank interest on Foxy Partnership K-1	1,600

Dividends

Walnut Company	$ 850
Mutual funds, Greyline	1,250
Dividends on Foxy Partnership K-1	800
Dividend from Acme on a life insurance policy	1,450

Explanation

Please enter the total amount of taxable interest and dividends.

	A	B
1	Taxable interest	$3,900 [123]
2	Taxable dividends	$2,900 [123]

Row 1: $3,900

This information is taken from the facts given.

Greenpoint Bank	$1,300
Whitewater Savings & Loan	1,000
Interest from Schedule K-1	1,600
Total	$3,900

Note that the interest from the Washington County Bonds is tax-exempt municipal bond interest.

Row 2: $2,900

This information is taken from the facts given.

Walnut Company	$850
Greyline Fund	1,250
Dividends from Schedule K-1	800
Total	$2,900

Note that "dividends" on life insurance policies are not true taxable dividends. They are a reduction of the premium paid for the policy.

B   Gross Income

Task-Based Simulation 2: Schedule C Deductions

EXHIBITS

close all exhibits

📄 Information

Scroll down to complete all parts of this task.

Note: You will need the data provided in the exhibit to work this task.

Please indicate how much of each item is deductible on Dennis Green's Schedule C.

	A	B
1		**Amount Deductible**
2	Cost of goods sold $15,800.	123
3	Insurance (liability coverage) $1,200.	123
4	Wages $18,000, including $5,000 wages for Dennis.	123
5	Rent $12,000.	123
6	Self-employment tax, per Schedule SE, will be $1,950.	123
7	Office expenses $5,000.	123
8	Maintenance and repairs $1,750.	123
9	Travel expenses $2,800, including $800 for meals.	123
10	Depreciation $1,873 (per tax tables).	123

Information   ☒

Dennis and Kelly Green, ages 55 and 45, respectively, are married and file a joint income tax return. The information provided in the answer table pertains to Dennis Green's self-employment as a painter.

Explanation

Please indicate how much of each item is deductible on Dennis Green's Schedule C.

	A	B
1		Amount Deductible
2	Cost of goods sold $15,800.	$15,800 🔢
3	Insurance (liability coverage) $1,200.	$1,200 🔢
4	Wages $18,000, including $5,000 wages for Dennis.	$13,000 🔢
5	Rent $12,000.	$12,000 🔢
6	Self-employment tax, per Schedule SE, will be $1,950.	$0 🔢
7	Office expenses $5,000.	$5,000 🔢
8	Maintenance and repairs $1,750.	$1,750 🔢
9	Travel expenses $2,800, including $800 for meals.	$2,400 🔢
10	Depreciation $1,873 (per tax tables).	$1,873 🔢

Row 2: $15,800
Cost of goods sold is fully deductible as a business expense on Schedule C.

Row 3: $1,200
Liability insurance is fully deductible as a business expense on Schedule C.

Row 4: $13,000
Wages paid to employees are fully deductible as a business expense on Schedule C. The $5,000 paid to Dennis is considered to be a draw and not deductible wages. The remaining $13,000 is deductible.

Row 5: $12,000
Rent is fully deductible as a business expense on Schedule C.

Row 6: $0
The SE tax is an additional tax added to income tax on Page 2 of Form 1040. Half of the SE tax, $975, is deductible on Page 1 of Form 1040 as an adjustment for adjusted gross income and is not deductible as a business expense on Schedule C.

Row 7: $5,000
Office expenses are fully deductible as a business expense on Schedule C.

Row 8: $1,750
Repairs and Maintenance expense is fully deductible as a business expense on Schedule C.

Row 9: $2,400
The $2,800 includes $800 of meals. The other $2,000 is pure travel expense, which is deductible as a business expense. Business meals are only 50% deductible, which is $400. $2,000 + $400 = $2,400.

Row 10: $1,873
Depreciation is fully deductible as a business expense on Schedule C.

Notes

1 Passive Activities

Passive activities are activities in which a taxpayer does not materially participate (e.g., limited partnership interests, rental activities, S corporations, and most tax shelters). All supplemental income and/or loss items such as rental real estate, royalties, and certain K-1 passive income/loss items from partnerships, S corporations, and trusts are reported on Schedule E.

2 Rental Income

Rental income is computed as:

> Gross Rental Income
>
> Prepaid Rental Income
>
> Rent Cancellation Payment
>
> Improvement in lieu of Rent
>
> < Rental Expenses >
> _____
>
> Net Rental Income
>
> OR
>
> Net Rental Loss
> _____

3 Losses From Passive Activities

Net passive activity losses generally may not be deducted from other income. They are carried forward until offset by passive activity income or until the activity is disposed of (100 percent deductible in the year of disposition).

3.1 "Mom and Pop" Exception

Taxpayers may deduct up to $25,000 (per year) of net rental passive losses if they actively participate or manage the rental property and own more than 10 percent of the activity. The $25,000 is reduced by 50 percent of the excess of AGI over $100,000 and eliminated when AGI exceeds $150,000.

C Passive Activity Losses

Question 1   MCQ-09738

Sam rents his second home. During the current year, he reported a
$40,000 net loss from the rental. Assume Sam actively participates
in the rental activity and no phase-out limitations apply. What is the
greatest amount of the rental loss that Sam can deduct against ordinary
income in the current year?

    1. $25,000

    2. $40,000

    3. $0

    4. $5,000

Task-Based Simulations

Task-Based Simulation: Rental Property

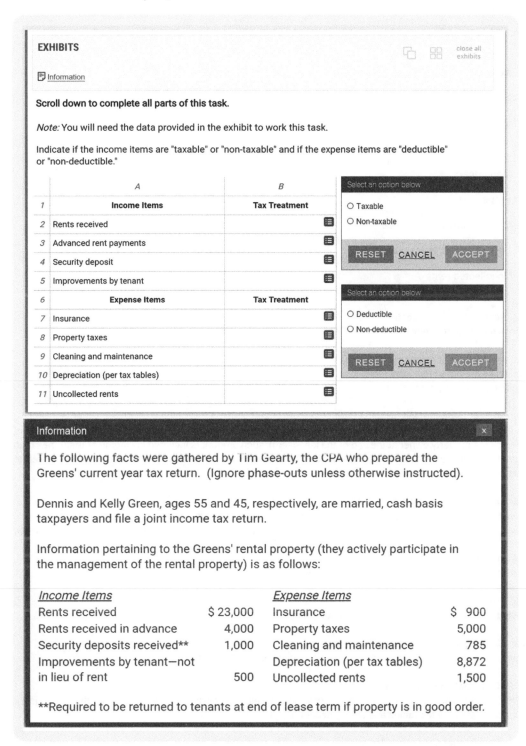

EXHIBITS

📄 Information

Scroll down to complete all parts of this task.

Note: You will need the data provided in the exhibit to work this task.

Indicate if the income items are "taxable" or "non-taxable" and if the expense items are "deductible" or "non-deductible."

	A	B	
1	**Income Items**	**Tax Treatment**	
2	Rents received		▤
3	Advanced rent payments		▤
4	Security deposit		▤
5	Improvements by tenant		▤
6	**Expense Items**	**Tax Treatment**	
7	Insurance		▤
8	Property taxes		▤
9	Cleaning and maintenance		▤
10	Depreciation (per tax tables)		▤
11	Uncollected rents		▤

Select an option below
- ○ Taxable
- ○ Non-taxable

RESET   CANCEL   ACCEPT

Select an option below
- ○ Deductible
- ○ Non-deductible

RESET   CANCEL   ACCEPT

Information   ✕

The following facts were gathered by Tim Gearty, the CPA who prepared the Greens' current year tax return. (Ignore phase-outs unless otherwise instructed).

Dennis and Kelly Green, ages 55 and 45, respectively, are married, cash basis taxpayers and file a joint income tax return.

Information pertaining to the Greens' rental property (they actively participate in the management of the rental property) is as follows:

Income Items		Expense Items	
Rents received	$ 23,000	Insurance	$ 900
Rents received in advance	4,000	Property taxes	5,000
Security deposits received**	1,000	Cleaning and maintenance	785
Improvements by tenant—not		Depreciation (per tax tables)	8,872
in lieu of rent	500	Uncollected rents	1,500

**Required to be returned to tenants at end of lease term if property is in good order.

C Passive Activity Losses

	A	B	
1	**Income Items**	**Tax Treatment**	
2	Rents received	Taxable	
3	Advanced rent payments	Taxable	
4	Security deposit	Non-taxable	
5	Improvements by tenant	Non-taxable	
6	**Expense Items**	**Tax Treatment**	
7	Insurance	Deductible	
8	Property taxes	Deductible	
9	Cleaning and maintenance	Deductible	
10	Depreciation (per tax tables)	Deductible	
11	Uncollected rents	Non-deductible	

Row 2: Rents received—Taxable
Proceeds received from renting real estate is taxable as rental income.

Row 3: Advanced rent payments—Taxable
Advanced payments of rent is included in income in the year received regardless of (i) the period covered or (ii) method of accounting used.

Row 4: Security deposit—Non-taxable
A security deposit is not income if the lessor is required to return it at the end of the lease term. If any amount is retained by the property owner at the end of the lease term, such amount is included in income at that time. If any portion of a security deposit is for the final month's rental payment, such amount is classified as advanced rental payments and would be included in income in the year received.

Row 5: Improvements by tenant—Non-taxable
Improvements by the lessee that are not in lieu of rent does not create a taxable event to the property owner. However, if such improvements were in lieu of rent, such amount would be taxable income to the property owner.

Row 7: Insurance—Deductible
Insurance is an ordinary expense of rental property.

Row 8: Property taxes—Deductible
Property taxes are an ordinary expense of rental property.

Row 9: Cleaning and maintenance—Deductible
Cleaning, maintenance, and repairs are ordinary expenses of rental property.

Row 10: Depreciation—Deductible
The IRS sets forth various depreciation tables for various types of property. Per the facts above, the $8,872 is the amount calculated per the tables and thus is deductible.

Row 11: Uncollected rents—Non-deductible
A cash method taxpayer may not deduct uncollected rents (or any other "bad debt" with respect to uncollected cash basis accounts receivables) because such amounts have not been included in income.

1 Adjustments to Gross Income

Adjustments are subtracted from gross income to arrive at adjusted gross income (reported on Form 1040, page 1).

1.1 Alimony Paid

Alimony paid for a divorce or separation agreement executed on or before 12/31/18 is an adjustment to gross income and alimony received is income.

1.2 Retirement Plan Contributions

1.2.1 Deductible Contributions to Traditional IRAs

Both of the following conditions must be met:

■ 2018 AGI does not exceed $63,000–$73,000 (S) or $101,000–$121,000 (MFJ). For 2019, AGI cannot exceed $64,000–$74,000 (S) or $103,000–$123,000 (MFJ).

■ The taxpayer does not actively participate in another qualified plan. (A spouse is not deemed to participate just because the other spouse participates, but this phases out with AGI between $189,000 and $199,000 for 2018 and with AGI between $193,000 and $203,000 for 2019.)

1.2.2 Maximum Deductible Amount

The maximum deductions for 2018 and 2019 are the lesser of $5,500 and $6,000, respectively, or the individual's compensation. (An individual over age 50 can make a $1,000 "catch-up contribution" in 2018 and 2019.)

■ For 2019, married taxpayers can contribute $12,000 ($6,000 each) provided combined earnings are greater than $12,000 (and other requirements are met).

Rules Summary: Traditional IRA							
Earned Income		Pension		Modified AGI		IRA	
Spouse 1	Spouse 2	Spouse 1	Spouse 2	2018	2019	Spouse 1	Spouse 2
Yes	Yes	No	No	Unlimited	Unlimited	Yes	Yes
Yes	No	No	N/A	Unlimited	Unlimited	Yes	Yes
Yes	No	Yes	N/A	Under $101,000	Under $103,000	Yes	Yes
Yes	No	Yes	N/A	$121,000–$189,000	$123,000–$193,000	No	Yes
Yes	No	Yes	N/A	Over $199,000	Over $203,000	No	No

IRA Summary			
	Deductible Traditional IRA	Nondeductible Traditional IRA	Roth IRA
Maximum contribution (2019):	$6,000 combined annual maximum contribution with $1,000 additional "catch up" contribution for ages 50 up to 70½; $0 for ages over 70½ (for traditional IRA only)		
Above-the-line deduction for contribution:	Yes	No	No
Withdrawals: • Contributions • Earnings	Taxable Taxable	Nontaxable Taxable	Nontaxable Nontaxable (if qualified distribution)

1.2.3 Nondeductible Contributions for 2018 and 2019

■ **Traditional Nondeductible IRAs:** For 2019, maximum contribution is lesser of $6,000, individual's earned income, or the amount not contributed to other IRAs.

■ **Roth IRAs:** The contribution limits are the same. For 2018, eligibility phases out for taxpayers with modified AGI between $120,000–$135,000 (S) and $189,000–$199,000 (MFJ). For 2019, eligibility phases out for taxpayers with modified AGI between $122,000–$137,000 (S) and $193,000–$203,000 (MFJ).

1.2.4 Keogh Plans

A self-employed taxpayer subject to the self-employment tax is generally allowed to set up a Keogh plan. The maximum contribution is limited to the lesser of:

■ $55,000 for 2018 and $56,000 for 2019; or

■ 25 percent of Keogh net earnings from self-employment.

Business Income

< Business Expenses >

Net Business Income

< 1/2 Self-Employment Tax >

< Keogh Deduction >

Keogh Net Earnings

1.3 Education Loan Interest (Qualified)

Limit of $2,500: For 2018, income phase-out levels are $65,000–$80,000 (S) and $135,000–$165,000 (MFJ). For 2019, income phase-out levels are $70,000–$85,000 (S) and $140,000–$170,000 (MFJ).

1.4   Educator Expenses

A deduction of up to $250 per eligible educator is allowed as an adjustment for qualified teaching/classroom expenses.

1.5   Moving Expenses

Starting in 2018, moving expense deductions are only allowed for members of the armed forces (or spouses and dependents) on active duty who move pursuant to a military order and incident to a permanent change of station.

1.6   Health Savings Accounts (HSA)

Health savings accounts allow employees with high-deductible insurance plans to make pretax contributions to an HSA to cover health care costs.

- Workers with high-deductible health insurance may make pretax contributions to cover health care costs. For 2019, the maximum contributions are $3,500 for single people and $7,000 for families. The plan deductible must be at least $1,350 ($2,700 for families), and the amount is indexed for inflation.

- Monies grow tax-free, and there is no time limit for spending.

- Withdrawals used to pay qualified medical expenses are excluded from gross income.

1.7   Other Adjustments

- Interest penalty on early withdrawal of funds.

- Self-employed health insurance premiums (100 percent deductible).

- Tax on self-employment income.

Question 1   MCQ-09451

Darwood and Samantha Stevens were divorced in January 2018. In accordance with the divorce decree, Darwood transferred title in their home to Samantha in 2018. The home, which had a fair market value of $300,000 was subject to a $100,000 mortgage that had more than 20 years to run. Monthly mortgage payments amount to $2,000. Under the terms of the settlement, Darwood is obligated to make the mortgage payments on the home for the full remaining 20-year term of the indebtedness, regardless of how long Samantha lives. Darwood made 12 mortgage payments in 2019. What amount is deductible by Darwood as alimony on his 2019 tax return?

1. $0
2. $24,000
3. $200,000
4. $224,000

---

2 Deductions From Adjusted Gross Income (AGI)

Taxpayers may generally choose between using the standard deduction and itemizing deductions. (This usually depends upon which produces the better tax result; however, if the taxpayer is MFS and his or her spouse itemizes deductions, the taxpayer must also itemize deductions).

2.1 Standard Deductions

	2018	2019
Single (MFS)	$12,000	$12,200
Head of Household	$18,000	$18,350
MFJ (or surviving spouse)	$24,000	$24,400

The additional standard deduction for those who are elderly or blind is $1,600 for 2018 and $1,650 for 2019 for single or head of household. For married taxpayers, the additional standard deduction amount is $1,300 in 2018 and $1,300 in 2019.

2.2 Itemized Deductions (Schedule A)

2.2.1 Medical Expenses

Medically necessary items (e.g., prescriptions, doctors, medical and accident insurance, and required surgery) are deductible on Schedule A, subject to 10 percent of AGI in 2019. Nondeductible expenses include elective/cosmetic surgery, life insurance, vitamins, etc.

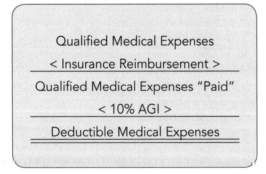

Qualified Medical Expenses
< Insurance Reimbursement >
Qualified Medical Expenses "Paid"
< 10% AGI >
Deductible Medical Expenses

2.2.2 State, Local, and Foreign Taxes

Real estate taxes, income taxes, and personal property taxes paid during the year are deductible up to an aggregate amount of $10,000. Federal taxes are not deductible.

2.2.3 Sales Tax

Sales taxes paid can be deducted instead of state and local income taxes (whichever is higher). The deduction is based on an IRS table or the actual substantiated sales tax.

2.2.4 Home Mortgage Interest

Qualified residence interest on a first or second home is deductible (both acquisition indebtedness and home equity indebtedness are included).

- **Acquisition:** Interest on up to $750,000 ($375,000 MFS) borrowed to construct, acquire, and improve a home.
- **Home Equity:** As part of the overall limit on total debt ($750,000 for 2019), interest from a home equity line used to construct or substantially improve the residence may be deducted.

2.2.5 Investment Interest

The deduction is limited to net (taxable) investment income. Interest incurred for tax-free investments is nondeductible.

2.2.6 Charitable Contributions

The maximum deduction for contributions to public charities is 60 percent of AGI for cash contributions (30 percent AGI for long-term capital gain property contributions). Contributions must be to qualified charities (i.e., gifts to individuals and political contributions are not deductible).

- Long-term appreciated property is deductible at the property's fair market value (no capital gain applies).
- Excess contributions can be carried forward for up to five years.
- Contribution of services is nondeductible, but the out-of-pocket expenses are deductible.

2.2.7 Casualty Losses

Applicable to nonbusiness property located in a federally declared disaster area.

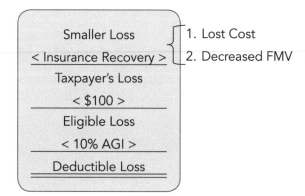

2.2.8 Miscellaneous Itemized Deductions

- Gambling losses are deductible to the extent of gambling winnings (reported on Form 1040, page 1).

- Federal estate tax paid on income in respect of a decedent.

- This is estate tax that was paid by an individual because of income received by the individual as a beneficiary of an estate. The federal estate tax paid (on Form 706) that related to the value of this income item is an allowable deduction for income tax purposes.

2.3 Qualified Business Income Deduction

The qualified business income (QBI) deduction (also known as the Section 199A deduction) is a deduction of up to 20 percent of qualified business income for eligible flow-through entities. The deduction is taken "below the line" or from adjusted gross income.

2.3.1 Definitions

1. **Qualified Business Income (QBI):** Ordinary income less ordinary deductions earned from a sole proprietorship, S corporation, limited liability company, or partnership connected to business conducted within the United States.

2. **Qualified Property:** Any tangible, depreciable property that is held by the business at the end of the year and is used at any point during the year in the production of QBI.

3. **Qualified Trade or Business (QTB):** Any business other than a specified service trade or business (SSTB).

4. **Specified Service Trade or Business (SSTB):** An SSTB is a trade or business involving direct services in certain fields (such as health, law, accounting, actuarial science, performing arts, consulting, athletics, financial services, and brokerage), and any trade in which the principal asset is the reputation or skill of one or more of its employees or owners. Engineering and architectural services are specifically excluded from the definition of SSTB.

2.3.2 Calculating the Deduction

The basic deduction:

20% × Qualified business income (QBI)

2.3.3 Limitations to the QBI Deduction

Limitations are applied to the QBI deduction based on the taxable income of the taxpayer and whether the business is a QTB or an SSTB. SSTBs are only eligible for the deduction if the taxpayer's taxable income is below a certain level.

Once the tentative QBI deduction is calculated, an overall limitation based on the taxpayer's taxable income in excess of net capital gain must be considered. The Section 199A QBI deduction is the lesser of:

1. Combined QBI deduction for all qualifying businesses; or

2. 20 percent of the taxpayer's taxable income (before the QBI deduction) in excess of net capital gain.

For purposes of the Section 199A overall taxable income limitation, net capital gain includes the excess of net long-term capital gain (LTCG) over net short-term capital loss (STCL) and qualified dividend income.

Question 2   MCQ-09482

In the current year, Wells paid the following expenses:

Premiums on an insurance policy against loss of earnings due to sickness or accident.	$3,000
Physical therapy after spinal surgery.	2,000
Premium on an insurance policy that covers reimbursement for the cost of prescription drugs.	500

In the current year, Wells recovered $1,500 of the $2,000 that she paid for physical therapy through insurance reimbursement from a group medical policy paid for by her employer. Disregarding the adjusted gross income percentage threshold, what amount could be claimed on Wells' current year income tax return for medical expenses?

1. $4,000
2. $3,500
3. $1,000
4. $500

D Adjustments and Deductions to Arrive at Taxable Income

Task-Based Simulations

Task-Based Simulation 1: Deductions for AGI

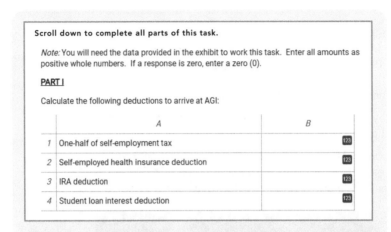

Scroll down to complete all parts of this task.

Note: You will need the data provided in the exhibit to work this task. Enter all amounts as positive whole numbers. If a response is zero, enter a zero (0).

<u>PART I</u>

Calculate the following deductions to arrive at AGI:

	A	B
1	One-half of self-employment tax	[123]
2	Self-employed health insurance deduction	[123]
3	IRA deduction	[123]
4	Student loan interest deduction	[123]

Information   ☒

The following facts were gathered by Tim Gearty, the CPA who prepared the Greens' current year tax return. (Ignore phase-outs unless otherwise instructed.)

1. Dennis and Kelly Green, ages 55 and 45, respectively, are married and file a joint income tax return. Dennis is employed by Olinto and Company, a corporation. Kelly is a grammar school teacher and is employed by the Douglas County School District. Dennis and Kelly live at 4 Jade Place, Green Acres, New York 47336.

   Their current year salary and withholdings were as follows:

Name	Social Security No.	Salaries	Social Security Tax	Medicare Tax	Federal Income Tax	State Income Tax
Dennis	111-22-3333	$30,000	$1,860	$435	$3,600	$1,480
Kelly	222-33-4444	14,000	868	203	1,200	1,240

2. The Greens have two children, Olive (age 16, SSN 333-44-5555) and Forrest (age 22, SSN 444-55-6666), both are full-time students at State University. Dennis and Kelly provide full support for both of their children.

3. Assume that self-employment tax, per Schedule SE, will be $1,975 from Dennis' self-employment income earned from the personal training he leads on the weekends.

4. Possible deductions:

   <u>Medical</u> *(for this issue: AGI = $90,000)*
   Self-employed health insurance 2,000

   <u>Taxes</u>
   Real estate:
       Residence .... $ 1,300
       Vacation home (Colorado) 900
   Personal property on tax calculated value of car 250
   Estimated payments, state income tax 800
   Estimated payments, federal income tax 3,400
   State sales taxes 500

   <u>Interest</u>
   Home mortgage interest:
   Residence .... $ 11,750
   Vacation home (never used as a rental) 4,350
   Unsecured auto loan 2,650
   Student loan interest (Kelly) 3,000

(continued)

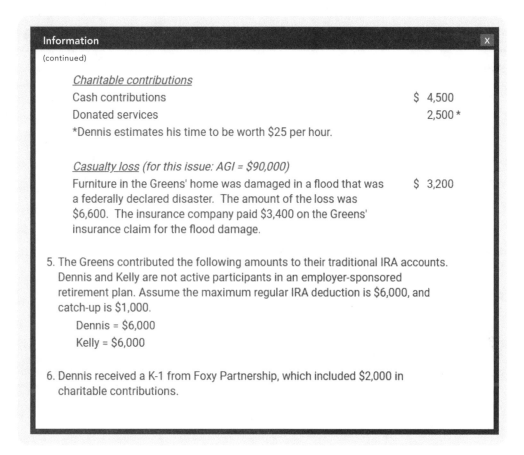

Information   [X]

(continued)

Charitable contributions

Cash contributions	$ 4,500
Donated services	2,500 *

*Dennis estimates his time to be worth $25 per hour.

Casualty loss (for this issue: AGI = $90,000)

Furniture in the Greens' home was damaged in a flood that was $ 3,200
a federally declared disaster. The amount of the loss was
$6,600. The insurance company paid $3,400 on the Greens'
insurance claim for the flood damage.

5. The Greens contributed the following amounts to their traditional IRA accounts.
Dennis and Kelly are not active participants in an employer-sponsored
retirement plan. Assume the maximum regular IRA deduction is $6,000, and
catch-up is $1,000.

   Dennis = $6,000
   Kelly = $6,000

6. Dennis received a K-1 from Foxy Partnership, which included $2,000 in
charitable contributions.

Explanation   X

PART I

	A	B
1	One-half of self-employment tax	$988 ▦
2	Self-employed health insurance deduction	$2,000 ▦
3	IRA deduction	$12,000 ▦
4	Student loan interest deduction	$2,500 ▦

Row 1: One-Half of Self-Employment Tax: $988
Self-employment tax (given) $1,975 × 50% = 988.

Row 2: Self-Employed Health Insurance Deduction: $2,000
Self-employed taxpayers may deduct 100% of their medical insurance premiums paid for themselves, spouse, and dependents.

Row 3: IRA Deduction: $12,000
An individual who is not an active participant in an employer-sponsored plan may deduct $6,000 for contributions to a traditional IRA. An individual who is age 50 or older is entitled to deduct an additional $1,000 catch-up contribution.

Dennis: $6,000
                     Note: Dennis could have contributed another $1,000 catch up if he desired.

Kelly: $6,000
Total: $12,000

Row 4: Student Loan Interest Expense: $2,500
Individuals may deduct as an adjustment toward AGI up to $2,500 of qualified student loan interest each year. This deduction is phased out for taxpayers with AGI of $135,000 to $165,000 (MFJ). The Greens' AGI is below this amount, so they are entitled to the full $2,500 deduction.

Task-Based Simulation 2: Itemized Deductions

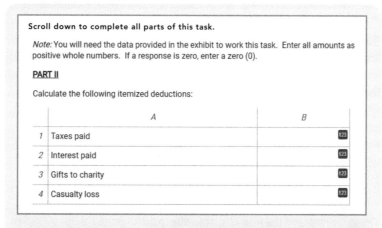

Scroll down to complete all parts of this task.

Note: You will need the data provided in the exhibit to work this task. Enter all amounts as positive whole numbers. If a response is zero, enter a zero (0).

PART II

Calculate the following itemized deductions:

	A	B
1	Taxes paid	123
2	Interest paid	123
3	Gifts to charity	123
4	Casualty loss	123

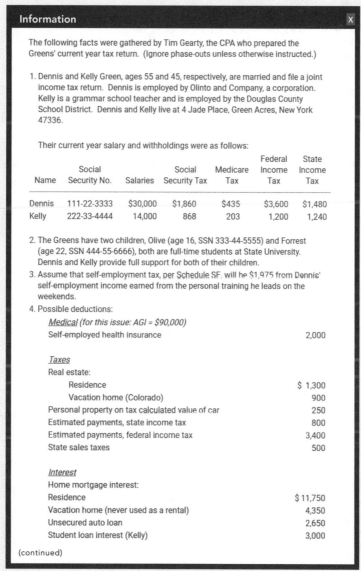

Information   X

The following facts were gathered by Tim Gearty, the CPA who prepared the Greens' current year tax return. (Ignore phase-outs unless otherwise instructed.)

1. Dennis and Kelly Green, ages 55 and 45, respectively, are married and file a joint income tax return. Dennis is employed by Olinto and Company, a corporation. Kelly is a grammar school teacher and is employed by the Douglas County School District. Dennis and Kelly live at 4 Jade Place, Green Acres, New York 47336.

Their current year salary and withholdings were as follows:

Name	Social Security No.	Salaries	Social Security Tax	Medicare Tax	Federal Income Tax	State Income Tax
Dennis	111-22-3333	$30,000	$1,860	$435	$3,600	$1,480
Kelly	222-33-4444	14,000	868	203	1,200	1,240

2. The Greens have two children, Olive (age 16, SSN 333-44-5555) and Forrest (age 22, SSN 444-55-6666), both are full-time students at State University. Dennis and Kelly provide full support for both of their children.

3. Assume that self-employment tax, per Schedule SE, will be $1,975 from Dennis' self-employment income earned from the personal training he leads on the weekends.

4. Possible deductions:

Medical (for this issue: AGI = $90,000)

Self-employed health insurance	2,000

Taxes

Real estate:

Residence	$ 1,300
Vacation home (Colorado)	900
Personal property on tax calculated value of car	250
Estimated payments, state income tax	800
Estimated payments, federal income tax	3,400
State sales taxes	500

Interest

Home mortgage interest:

Residence	$ 11,750
Vacation home (never used as a rental)	4,350
Unsecured auto loan	2,650
Student loan interest (Kelly)	3,000

(continued)

D Adjustments and Deductions to Arrive at Taxable Income

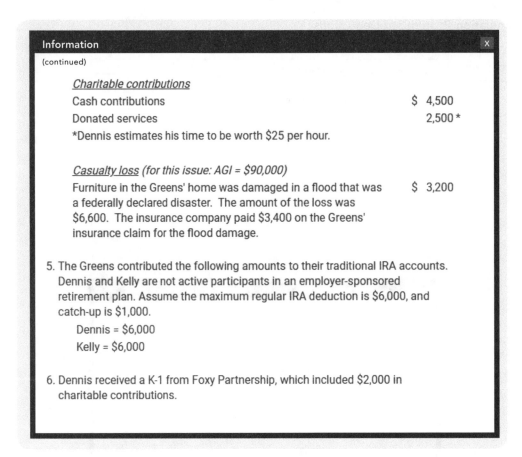

Information   ☒

(continued)

    Charitable contributions

Cash contributions	$ 4,500
Donated services	2,500 *

    *Dennis estimates his time to be worth $25 per hour.

    Casualty loss (for this issue: AGI = $90,000)

Furniture in the Greens' home was damaged in a flood that was a federally declared disaster. The amount of the loss was $6,600. The insurance company paid $3,400 on the Greens' insurance claim for the flood damage. $ 3,200

5. The Greens contributed the following amounts to their traditional IRA accounts. Dennis and Kelly are not active participants in an employer-sponsored retirement plan. Assume the maximum regular IRA deduction is $6,000, and catch-up is $1,000.

    Dennis = $6,000

    Kelly = $6,000

6. Dennis received a K-1 from Foxy Partnership, which included $2,000 in charitable contributions.

Explanation   ☒

PART II

	A	B
1	Taxes paid	$5,970 🔢
2	Interest paid	$16,100 🔢
3	Gifts to charity	$6,500 🔢
4	Casualty loss	$0 🔢

Row 1: Taxes Paid: $5,970
State withholding—Dennis = $1,480
State withholding—Kelly = $1,240
State estimated payments = $800
Federal income taxes are not deductible.
Real estate taxes—residence = $1,300
Real estate taxes—vacation home = $900
Personal property taxes—car = $250
Taxpayers may deduct state and local income taxes or state and local sales taxes, but not both.
The Greens' total state withholdings and estimated tax payments are greater than the state
sales taxes paid, so they would deduct the state income taxes rather than the state sales taxes.

Row 2: Interest Paid: $16,100
Home mortgage interest—residence = $11,750
Home mortgage interest—vacation home = $4,350
Interest paid on an unsecured auto loan is personal interest and not deductible.

Row 3: Gifts to Charity: $6,500
Cash contributions = $4,500
Contributions from Schedule K-1 = $2,000
*The donated services are not deductible as charitable contributions. Only out-of-pocket
expenses associated with donated services are deductible on Schedule A.*

Row 4: Casualty Losses: $0
Although the Greens incurred a federally declared disaster casualty loss, the deductible loss is
zero as only the portion which exceeds $100 and 10% of AGI is deductible.
Loss = $6,600
Insurance recovery = ($3,400)
Subtotal = $3,200
Reduction per occurrence = ($100)
Subtotal = $3,100
10% AGI = ($9,000)
No deductible loss as this is less than zero.

D Adjustments and Deductions to Arrive at Taxable Income

Task-Based Simulation 3: Research

Kelly is married and files a joint return with her husband. What code section and subsection describes the circumstances under which she can deduct a contribution to an individual retirement account (IRA)?

Enter your response in the answer fields below. Guidance on correctly structuring your response appears above and below the answer fields.

> ### Type the section here.
> *Examples of correctly formatted sections are shown below.*
>
> IRC § [   ] ([   ])
>
> ⓘ Examples of correctly formatted IRC responses are IRC§1(a), IRC§56(a), IRC§54A(a), IRC§162(a), IRC§54AA(a), IRC§263a(a), IRC§1245(a), IRC§2032a(a), IRC§1400U-1(a).

Explanation

Source of answer for this question:

IRC Section 219, Subsection (c)

Keywords: Spouse IRA contribution

1 Tax Computation

> Tax = Taxable income × Tax rate*
>
> *The rate is generally given on the exam.

2 Tax Credits

Tax credits reduce the calculated gross tax.

2.1 Child and Dependent Care Credit

- **Maximum Expenses:** $3,000 (one dependent); $6,000 (two or more).

- **Requirements:** Taxpayers must maintain a household, work, and incur eligible expenses for care of a qualifying child under age 13 (for whom an exemption can be claimed), any disabled dependent, or a spouse.

- **Eligible Expenses:** These include a babysitter and day care, but *not* school.

- **Computation of Credit:** Eligible expenses multiplied by 20–35 percent (specific credit percentage depends on AGI).

2.2 Child Tax Credit

- Credit of $2,000 per dependent child under age 17.

- Phased out at $200,000 (S) and $400,000 (MFJ).

- Partially refundable (i.e., can reduce tax below zero and result in a refund).

- A taxpayer may claim an additional nonrefundable tax credit of $500 for each dependent who is not a qualifying child under age 17. This may include children who are age 17 and older or other dependents who meet the requirements of a qualifying relative. The non-child dependent credit is subject to the same AGI phase-outs and is not refundable.

2.3   Credit for the Elderly and/or Permanently Disabled

Credit is equal to 15 percent of eligible income to individuals 65 years or older or less than 65 but permanently disabled.

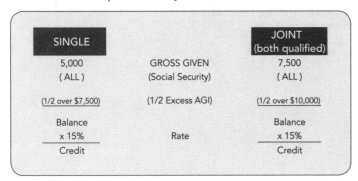

SINGLE	GROSS GIVEN	JOINT (both qualified)
5,000 (ALL)	(Social Security)	7,500 (ALL)
(1/2 over $7,500)	(1/2 Excess AGI)	(1/2 over $10,000)
Balance x 15%	Rate	Balance x 15%
Credit		Credit

2.4   Education Tax Incentives

Phased out for high-earning taxpayers.

2.4.1   American Opportunity Credit

Individuals are eligible during the first four years of college. For 2018 and 2019, this credit is a maximum of $2,500 (100 percent of the first $2,000, plus 25 percent of the next $2,000 expenses).

2.4.2   Lifetime Learning Credit

This credit is available for an unlimited number of years. It is equal to 20 percent of qualified expenses of up to $10,000.

2.5   Retirement Plan Contribution Credit

Up to $1,000 for traditional or Roth IRA contributions.

2.6   Earned Income Credit

The earned income credit is a *refundable* credit for low-income taxpayers.

■ The taxpayer must live in the U.S. for more than half the taxable year and meet certain low-income thresholds and other requirements.

■ The maximum basic earned income credit is between 7.65 and 40 percent of earned income, depending upon filing status and the number of dependents (note that having zero dependents does not preclude claiming the earned income credit).

2.7 Foreign Tax Credit

The credit is limited to the *lesser* of:

- Foreign taxes paid; or:

$$\frac{\text{Taxable income from all foreign operations}}{\text{Total taxable income from U.S. and foreign sources}} \times \text{U.S. tax}$$

- Any excess credit is either carried back one year and/or carried forward ten years.

Question 1   MCQ-09578

Which of the following credits is considered "refundable"?

1. Child and dependent care credit.

2. Retirement plan contribution credit.

3. Child tax credit.

4. Credit for elderly.

---

3 Estimated Tax

A taxpayer is required to make estimated quarterly tax payments if both of the following conditions are met:

1. $1,000 or more remaining tax liability (after withholding is applied).

2. Withholding (and estimated tax payments) is less than the lesser of:

- 90 percent of current year tax; or

- 100 percent of prior year tax [110 percent when the taxpayer's AGI is in excess of $150,000 (MFJ)].

4 Extensions of Time to File

When a taxpayer files a timely Form 4868 (by the original due date of the return—usually April 15), the taxpayer will receive an automatic six-month extension of time to file (but not time to pay) his or her income tax return.

Notes

Alternative Minimum Tax

1 Alternative Minimum Tax Computation

Alternative minimum tax is a parallel tax system to the regular tax system. It calculates a minimum amount of tax to be paid by certain taxpayers in any given year. The calculation begins with regular taxable income and adjusts it according to the alternative minimum tax rules. The taxpayer will have to pay "Alt Min" tax when his or her tentative minimum tax (calculated under the alternative minimum tax rules) exceeds his or her regular tax (calculated under the regular tax rules).

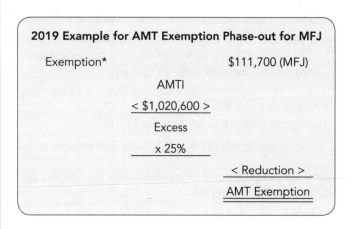

```
        Regular Taxable Income
              ± Adjustments
              + Preferences
   Alternative Minimum Taxable Income
             < Exemption >
     Alternative Minimum Tax Base
            × Tax Computation
           Tentative AMT Tax
             < Tax Credits >
        Tentative Minimum Tax
         < Regular Income Tax >
       Alternative Minimum Tax
```

2019 Example for AMT Exemption Phase-out for MFJ

Exemption*	$111,700 (MFJ)
AMTI	
< $1,020,600 >	
Excess	
x 25%	
	< Reduction >
	AMT Exemption

*For 2018, the exemption amounts are $109,400 (MFJ), $70,300 (H of H and single), and $54,700 (MFS). For 2019, the exemption amounts are $111,700 (MFJ), $71,700 (H of H and single), and $55,850 (MFS). 2018 income thresholds for the phase-out are $1,000,000 (MFJ), $500,000 (H of H and single) and $500,000 (MFS). 2019 income thresholds for the phase-out are $1,020,600 (MFJ), $510,300 (H of H and single), and $510,300 (MFS).

1.1 Adjustments

Adjustments represent mainly timing differences (income is recognized sooner under alternative minimum tax rules). [**PANIC TS**]

- **P**assive activity losses are added back or recalculated.

- **A**ccelerated depreciation (post-1986 purchases) has an adjustment for the difference between tax and straight-line for real property and between tax and 150 percent declining balance for personal property.

- **N**et operating loss of the individual taxpayer is recomputed.

- **I**nstallment income of a dealer is an adjustment because the installment method is not allowed for AMT.

- **C**ontracts: Percentage completion versus completed contract.

- **T**axes are added back.
- **S**tandard deductions are disallowed.

1.2   Tax Preferences (Always Add-Backs)

- Private activity bond tax-exempt interest (with exceptions).
- Pre-1987 accelerated depreciation on real property and leased personal property.
- Percentage depletion deduction (excess over adjusted basis of property).

1.3   AMT Credit

- If a taxpayer pays alternative minimum tax, a credit against future regular tax is granted for the amount of alternative minimum tax paid (with some exceptions). The carryforward of this credit is indefinite.

Question 1	MCQ-09530

In the current year, Stan and Virginia Silver had $82,000 of taxable income. The Silvers, who were both age 66, had no tax preferences. The Silvers itemized deductions were as follows:

State and local income taxes	$ 3,000
Home mortgage interest to acquire the house	9,000
Home equity interest not used to buy or build the house	3,000

What amount did the Silvers report as alternative minimum taxable income before the AMT exemption?

1. $82,000
2. $85,000
3. $94,250
4. $97,250

V Federal Taxation of Entities

1 Book Income vs. Taxable Income

The following chart gives an overview of the differences between financial and tax accounting for corporations.

Corporation Tax Summary	GAAP: Financial Statements	IRC: Tax Return	Temp.	Perm.	None
Gross Income					
Gross sales	Income	Income			✓
Installment sales	Income	Income when received	✓		
Rents and royalties in advance	Income when earned	Income when received	✓		
State tax refund	Income	Income			✓
Dividends: equity method 100/65/50% exclusion	Income is subsidiary's earnings No exclusion	Income is dividends-received Excluded forever	✓	✓	
Items Not Includable in "Taxable Income"					
State and municipal bond interest	Income	Not taxable income		✓	
Life insurance proceeds	Income	Generally not taxable income		✓	
Gain/loss on treasury stock	Not reported	Not reported			✓
Ordinary Expenses					
Cost of goods sold	Currently expensed	Uniform capitalization rules			✓
Officers' compensation (top)	Expense	$1,000,000 limit			✓
Bad debt	Allowance (estimated)	Direct write-off	✓		
Estimated liability for contingency (e.g., warranty)	Expense (accrue estimated)	No deduction until paid	✓		
Interest expense: business loan	Expense	Deduct			✓
Tax-free investment	Expense	Not deductible		✓	
Contributions	All expensed	Limited to 10% of adjusted taxable income	✓	✓	✓
Loss on abandonment/casualty	Expense	Deduct			✓
Loss on worthless subsidiary	Expense	Deduct			✓
Depreciation: MACRS vs. straight-line	Slow depreciation	Fast depreciation	✓		
Section 179 depreciation	Not allowed (must depreciate)	2019: $1,020,000	✓		
Different basis of asset	Use GAAP basis	Use tax basis		✓	
Amortization: start-up/organizational expenses	Expense	$5,000 maximum/15 year excess	✓		
Franchise	Amortize	Amortize over 15 years	✓		
Goodwill	Impairment test	Amortize over 15 years	✓		
Depletion: percentage vs. straight-line (cost)	Cost over years	Percentage of sales	✓		
Percentage in excess of cost	Not allowed	Percentage of sales		✓	
Profit sharing and pension expense	Expense accrued	No deduction until paid	✓		
Accrued expense (50% owner/family)	Expense accrued	No deduction until paid	✓		
State taxes (paid)	Expense	Deduct			✓
Meals	Expense	Generally 50% deductible		✓	

(continued on next page)

(continued)

GAAP Expense Items That Are Not Tax Deductions					
Life insurance expense (corporation)	Expense	Not deductible		✓	
Penalties	Expense	Not deductible		✓	
Lobbying/political expense	Expense	Not deductible		✓	
Federal income taxes	Expense	Not deductible		✓	
Entertainment expense	Expense	Not deductible		✓	
Special Items					
Net capital gain	Income	Income			✓
Net capital loss	Report as loss	Not deductible	✓		
Carryback/carryover (3 years back/5 years forward)	Not applicable	Unused loss allowed as a STCL	✓		
Related shareholder	Report as a loss	Not deductible		✓	
Net operating loss	Report as a loss	Carryover indefinitely	✓		
Research and development	Expense	Expense/amortize/capitalize	✓	✓	✓

Question 1   MCQ-09469

In Year 6, Garland Corp. contributed $40,000 to a qualified charitable organization. Garland's Year 6 taxable income before the deduction for charitable contributions was $410,000. Included in that amount is a $20,000 dividends-received deduction. Garland also had carryover contributions of $5,000 from the prior year. In Year 6, what amount can Garland deduct as charitable contributions?

1. $40,000
2. $41,000
3. $43,000
4. $45,000

Differences Between Book and Tax Income   A

		SCHEDULE M-1	

Reconciliation of Income (Loss) per Books to Taxable Income

1		Net Income (or loss) per Books	$875,000	7	– Income recorded on books this year not included on this return		
2	+	Federal Income Tax (per books)	$384,500		– Tax-exempt interest		$3,500
3	+	Excess Capital Losses over Gains	$5,000		– Life Insurance proceeds		$100,000
4	+	Income subject to tax not recorded on books this year					
	+	Installment Sale Income	$8,500				
	+	Rents Received in Advance	$15,000				
5	+	Expenses recorded on books this year not on the tax return		8	– Deductions on this return not charged against book income this year:		
	+	Book Depreciation	$14,000		– Tax Depreciation		$28,000
	+	Contribution Carryover	$0		– Contribution Carryover		$0
	+	Meals	$4,200		– Section 179 Deduction		$20,000
	+	Allowance for Doubtful Accts. (Incr.)	$15,000		– Direct Bad Debt Write-offs		$8,650
	+	Warranty Accrual	$8,500		– Actual Warranty Costs		$7,500
	+	Different Basis of Assets	$0		– Different Basis of Assets		$0
	+	Expense of Organizational Costs	$0		– Amortization of Organizational Cost		$500
	+	Goodwill Impairment per Books	$5,000		– Goodwill Amortization per Return		$9,200
	+	Pension Expense Accrued	$12,000		– Pensions Paid		$11,350
	+	Penalties	$1,000				
6		Add lines 1 through 5	$1,347,700	9	Add lines 7 and 8		$100,700
				10	Income (Line 28 Page 1) Line 6 minus Line 9		$1,159,000

This is taxable income per page 1 of the tax return, before the dividends received deduction and the NOL carryforward deduction.

A   Differences Between Book and Tax Income

Task-Based Simulations

Task-Based Simulation 1: M-1 Calculation

Information   [x]

Kristi Corp. is a calendar-year accrual-basis corporation that commenced operations on January 1, Year 1. The following adjusted accounts appear on Kristi's records for the year ended December 31, Year 10.

Revenues and gains	
Gross sales	$2,000,000
Interest:	
U.S. Treasury bonds	26,000
Municipal bonds	25,000
Life insurance proceeds—key person (director)	40,000
Gain on sale:	
Unimproved lot (1)	20,000
JLG stock (2)	5,000
State franchise tax refund	14,000
Total	$2,130,000

Costs and expenses	
Cost of goods sold	$ 350,000
Salaries and wages	470,000
Depreciation:	
Real property	50,000
Personal property	100,000
Bad debt (3)	10,000
State franchise tax	25,000
Vacation expense	10,000
Interest expense (4)	16,000
Life insurance premiums (5)	20,000
Federal income taxes	200,000
Business entertainment expense	20,000
Other operating expenses	29,000
Total	1,300,000
Net income	$ 830,000

Additional Information
(1) Gain on the sale of unimproved lot, purchased in Year 1 for use in business for $50,000. Sold in Year 10 for $70,000. Kristi Corp. has never had any Section 1231 losses.
(2) Gain on sale of JLG Stock, purchased in Year 1.
(3) Bad Debt: Represents the increase in the allowance for doubtful accounts based on an aging of accounts receivable. Actual bad debts written off were $7,000. Kristi Corp. recovered $2,000 of an account from prior years' bad debt. The account had been written off for tax purposes and had reduced Kristi's income tax liability.
(4) Interest expense on:

Mortgage loan	$10,000
Loan obtained to purchase municipal	
bonds	4,000
Operating line of credit loan	2,000

(5) Life insurance premiums paid by the Corporation for its employees as part of their compensation. The Corporation is not the beneficiary.

Differences Between Book and Tax Income   A

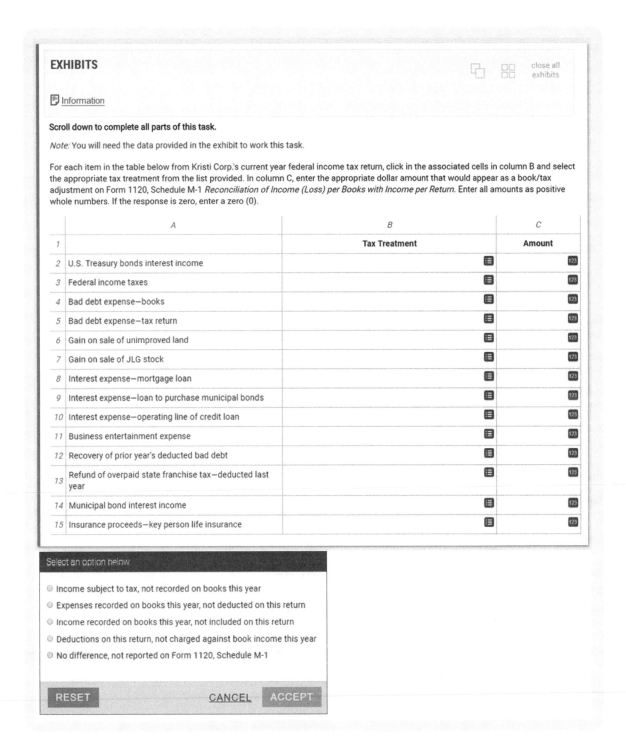

EXHIBITS   close all exhibits

📄 Information

Scroll down to complete all parts of this task.

Note: You will need the data provided in the exhibit to work this task.

For each item in the table below from Kristi Corp.'s current year federal income tax return, click in the associated cells in column B and select the appropriate tax treatment from the list provided. In column C, enter the appropriate dollar amount that would appear as a book/tax adjustment on Form 1120, Schedule M-1 *Reconciliation of Income (Loss) per Books with Income per Return.* Enter all amounts as positive whole numbers. If the response is zero, enter a zero (0).

	A	B	C
1		**Tax Treatment**	**Amount**
2	U.S. Treasury bonds interest income	📋	123
3	Federal income taxes	📋	123
4	Bad debt expense—books	📋	123
5	Bad debt expense—tax return	📋	123
6	Gain on sale of unimproved land	📋	123
7	Gain on sale of JLG stock	📋	123
8	Interest expense—mortgage loan	📋	123
9	Interest expense—loan to purchase municipal bonds	📋	123
10	Interest expense—operating line of credit loan	📋	123
11	Business entertainment expense	📋	123
12	Recovery of prior year's deducted bad debt	📋	123
13	Refund of overpaid state franchise tax—deducted last year	📋	123
14	Municipal bond interest income	📋	123
15	Insurance proceeds—key person life insurance	📋	123

Select an option below

○ Income subject to tax, not recorded on books this year

○ Expenses recorded on books this year, not deducted on this return

○ Income recorded on books this year, not included on this return

○ Deductions on this return, not charged against book income this year

○ No difference, not reported on Form 1120, Schedule M-1

RESET   CANCEL   ACCEPT

Regulation Final Review   **V   A-5**

Explanation

Row 2: No difference, not reported on Form 1120, Schedule M-1 | $0
Interest income from U.S. Treasury bonds is taxable. The full $26,000 is included in taxable income.

Row 3: Expenses recorded on books this year, not deducted on this return | $200,000
Federal income taxes are not deductible.

Row 4: Expenses recorded on books this year, not deducted on this return | $10,000
The allowance method of calculating bad debt expense is not permitted for federal income tax purposes.

Row 5: Deductions on this return, not charged against book income this year | $7,000
The direct write-off method is used for tax purposes to deduct bad debts actually written-off.

Row 6: No difference, not reported on Form 1120, Schedule M-1 | $0
Gain on the sale of real property (unimproved land) is included in taxable income. The net long-term capital gain is calculated as follows:

Sale price	$ 70,000
Cost (adjusted basis)	(50,000)
Gain	$ 20,000

Row 7: No difference, not reported on Form 1120, Schedule M-1 | $0
Gain on the sale of JLG Corp. stock is fully includible in taxable income. The $5,000 gain is correctly included in taxable income.

Row 8: No difference, not reported on Form 1120, Schedule M-1 | $0
The $10,000 of mortgage loan interest is deductible on the tax return.

Row 9: Expenses recorded on books this year, not deducted on this return | $4,000
Interest on a loan to purchase municipal bonds is not deductible because municipal bond interest income is not included in taxable income.

Row 10: No difference, not reported on Form 1120, Schedule M-1 | $0
The $2,000 of interest on the operating line of credit loan is tax deductible.

Row 11: Expenses recorded on books this year, not deducted on this return | $20,000
Business entertainment expenses are not deductible as ordinary and necessary business expenses.

Row 12: Income subject to tax, not recorded on books this year | $2,000
Recovery of an account receivable previously written off for tax purposes is fully taxable.

Row 13: No difference, not reported on Form 1120, Schedule M-1 | $0
Refund of state franchise tax overpayment previously deducted is fully taxable. The $14,000 is correctly included in taxable income.

Row 14: Income recorded on books this year, not included on this return | $25,000
Municipal bond interest is not taxable for regular tax purposes.

Row 15: Income recorded on books this year, not included on this return | $40,000
Key person life insurance proceeds are not taxable.

Task-Based Simulation 2: Book Vs. Tax

Information   ☒

Kristi Corp. is a calendar-year accrual-basis corporation that commenced operations on January 1, Year 1. The following adjusted accounts appear on Kristi's records for the year ended December 31, Year 10.

Revenues and gains	
Gross sales	$2,000,000
Interest:	
U.S. Treasury bonds	26,000
Municipal bonds	25,000
Life insurance proceeds—key person (director)	40,000
Gain on sale:	
Unimproved lot (1)	20,000
JLG stock (2)	5,000
State franchise tax refund	14,000
Total	$2,130,000

Costs and expenses	
Cost of goods sold	$ 350,000
Salaries and wages	470,000
Depreciation:	
Real property	50,000
Personal property	100,000
Bad debt (3)	10,000
State franchise tax	25,000
Vacation expense	10,000
Interest expense (4)	16,000
Life insurance premiums (5)	20,000
Federal income taxes	200,000
Business entertainment expense	20,000
Other operating expenses	29,000
Total	1,300,000
Net income	$ 830,000

Additional Information

(1) Gain on the sale of unimproved lot, purchased in Year 1 for use in business for $50,000. Sold in Year 10 for $70,000. Kristi Corp. has never had any Section 1231 losses.

(2) Gain on sale of JLG Stock, purchased in Year 1.

(3) Bad Debt: Represents the increase in the allowance for doubtful accounts based on an aging of accounts receivable. Actual bad debts written off were $7,000. Kristi Corp. recovered $2,000 of an account from prior years' bad debt. The account had been written off for tax purposes and had reduced Kristi's income tax liability.

(4) Interest expense on:

Mortgage loan	$10,000
Loan obtained to purchase municipal bonds	4,000
Operating line of credit loan	2,000

(5) Life insurance premiums paid by the Corporation for its employees as part of their compensation. The Corporation is not the beneficiary.

A Differences Between Book and Tax Income

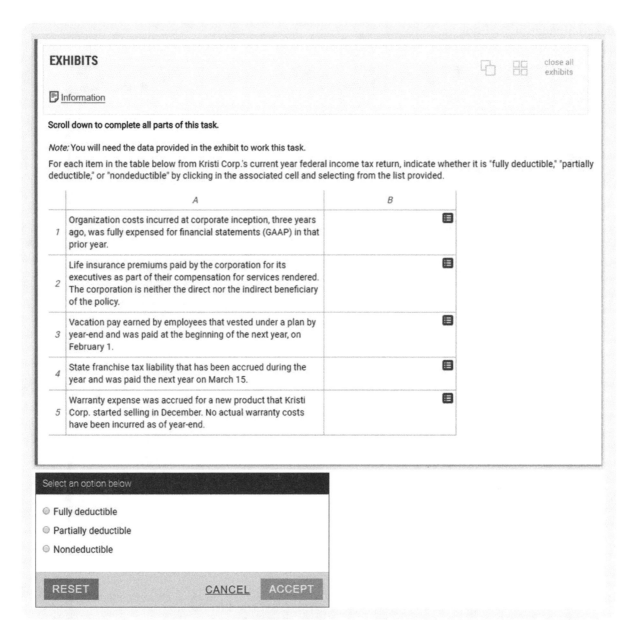

EXHIBITS

close all exhibits

📄 Information

Scroll down to complete all parts of this task.

Note: You will need the data provided in the exhibit to work this task.

For each item in the table below from Kristi Corp.'s current year federal income tax return, indicate whether it is "fully deductible," "partially deductible," or "nondeductible" by clicking in the associated cell and selecting from the list provided.

	A	B
1	Organization costs incurred at corporate inception, three years ago, was fully expensed for financial statements (GAAP) in that prior year.	☰
2	Life insurance premiums paid by the corporation for its executives as part of their compensation for services rendered. The corporation is neither the direct nor the indirect beneficiary of the policy.	☰
3	Vacation pay earned by employees that vested under a plan by year-end and was paid at the beginning of the next year, on February 1.	☰
4	State franchise tax liability that has been accrued during the year and was paid the next year on March 15.	☰
5	Warranty expense was accrued for a new product that Kristi Corp. started selling in December. No actual warranty costs have been incurred as of year-end.	☰

Select an option below

○ Fully deductible

○ Partially deductible

○ Nondeductible

RESET   CANCEL   ACCEPT

Explanation   x

Row 1: Partially deductible
Up to $5,000 of organizational expenditures (and up to $5,000 of start-up costs separately) may have been deducted in the start-up year. However, the $5,000 would have been reduced by the amount organizational expenditures (start-up costs, separately) exceeded $50,000. Any excess would then be amortized over 180 months (beginning with the month the active trade or business begins).

Row 2: Fully deductible
Life insurance premiums paid by the corporation for its executives as part of their compensation for services rendered is fully deductible when the corporation is not a beneficiary, directly or indirectly.

Row 3: Fully deductible
Vacation pay earned by employees that vested under a plan and was paid within 2½ months after year-end is fully deductible.

Row 4: Fully deductible
The state franchise tax liability that was accrued during the year and was paid on March 15 of the next year is fully deductible.

Row 5: Nondeductible
Although allowances for contingent liabilities are accrued for GAAP financial statements, contingent liability allowances are generally not deductible for income tax purposes until the actual contingent liability is paid (such as payment of an actual warranty claim).

Notes

1 Corporate Formation

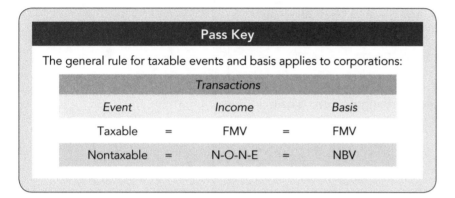

The general rule for taxable events and basis applies to corporations:

Transactions				
Event		*Income*		*Basis*
Taxable	=	FMV	=	FMV
Nontaxable	=	N-O-N-E	=	NBV

1.1 Corporation Tax Consequences

1.1.1 No Gain or Loss Recognized

There is no gain or loss recognized when the corporation issues stock in exchange for property in the following transactions: (1) formation; (2) purchase of treasury stock; and (3) resale of treasury stock.

1.1.2 Basis of Property (Corporation Receives)

The basis of the property received from the transferor/shareholder is the greater of:

■ the adjusted basis (net book value) of the shareholder plus any gain recognized by the shareholder; or

■ debt assumed by the corporation.

1.2 Shareholder Tax Consequences

1.2.1 No Gain or Loss Recognized

Shareholders will not recognize gain or loss if the following conditions have been met:

■ 80 percent control (must exist immediately after the transaction).

■ No boot is received by the shareholder.

The following items represent (taxable) boot and/or will trigger gain recognition:

• Cash withdrawn.

• COD (cancellation of debt)—The amount of liabilities that exceed the net book value of assets transferred into the corporation is not boot but generates gain.

Question 1   MCQ-09516

Gearty and Olinto organized The Worthington Corp., which issued voting common stock with a fair market value of $240,000. They each transferred property in exchange for stock as follows:

	Property	Adjusted Basis	Fair-Market Value	Percentage of the Worthington Corp. Stock Acquired
Gearty	Building	$80,000	$164,000	60%
Olinto	Land	$10,000	$ 96,000	40%

The building was subject to a $20,000 mortgage that was assumed by the Worthington Corp. What was The Worthington Corp.'s basis in the building?

1. $60,000
2. $80,000
3. $144,000
4. $104,000

2 Taxation of a C Corporation

2.1 Tax Calculation and Double Taxation

Corporations pay income tax at the corporate level at a flat tax rate of 21 percent. Dividends paid to the shareholders are also subject to tax at the shareholder level, thus creating the concept of double taxation.

2.2 Estimated Payments of Corporate Tax

- Corporations other than large corporations pay the lower of:
  - 100 percent of the tax shown on the return for the current year; or
  - 100 percent of the tax shown on the return for the preceding year.

- Large corporations must pay 100 percent of the tax as shown on the current year return

2.3 Dividends Received Deduction

In an attempt to prevent triple taxation of earnings, domestic corporations (those that are not personal service corporations, personal holding companies, or personally taxed S corporations) are allowed a "dividends received deduction." The amount of this deduction depends on the percentage that the corporation owns of the investee corporation that paid the dividends.

Percentage Ownership	Dividends Received Deduction
0% to < 20%	50%
20% to < 80%	65%
80% to 100%	100%

2.4 Net Operating Losses (NOL)

Beginning in 2018, corporations are allowed to carry forward net operating losses indefinitely. However, a net operating loss deducted in a single year may not exceed 80 percent of taxable income prior to the NOL deduction.

2.5 Consolidated Returns

An affiliated group of corporations may elect to be taxed as a single unit, thereby eliminating intercompany gains and losses. An affiliated group means that a common parent directly owns:

1. 80 percent or more of the voting power of all outstanding stock; and

2. 80 percent or more of the value of all outstanding stock of each corporation.

Note

Not all corporations are allowed the privilege of filing a consolidated return. Examples of those that are denied the privilege include S corporations, foreign corporations, most real estate investment trusts (REITs), some insurance companies, and most exempt organizations.

Question 2   MCQ-09484

In Year 6, Acorn Inc. had the following items of income and expense:

Sales	$500,000
Cost of sales	250,000
Dividends received	25,000

The dividends were received from a corporation of which Acorn owns 30%. In Acorn's Year 6 corporate income tax return, what amount should be reported as income before special deductions?

1. $525,000
2. $505,000
3. $275,000
4. $250,000

3 Corporate Earnings and Profits (E&P)

3.1 General

- Required for corporate income tax return preparation.

- The starting point is corporate taxable income.

- Affect corporate distributions and other activities—E&P is:

  - a major factor in determining the ability of the corporation to pay a dividend to the shareholders.

  - critical to the tax impact of corporate distributions, or nonliquidating dividends.

  - a factor in the determination of corporate reorganizations, accumulated earnings tax, stock redemptions, partial liquidations, and the tax status of certain S corporations that have previously been C corporations.

3.2 Accumulated Earnings and Profits

Generally, the amount of "Accumulated E&P" is the amount of E&P that exists as of the end of the tax year that precedes the current year. For any given year, the distinction between current E&P and accumulated E&P is necessary for the classification of corporate distributions.

3.2.1 General Calculation

The following formula is used to calculate the accumulated E&P to carry forward to the tax year after the current year:

> Accumulated E&P as of the beginning of the year
> Add/Subtract: Current E&P for the tax year less any distributions deemed from current E&P
> Subtract: Distributions from accumulated E&P
> Accumulated E&P as of the end of the year

3.2.2 Classification of Distribution

Corporate distributions are first applied to current E&P, then to accumulated E&P, and then to return of capital. If any excess remains, it is classified as "excess distributions" and reported as capital gain distributions (taxable income) by the shareholder. Distributions within the year are allocated based on the ratio of each distribution to the total distribution. Note that the allocation of the excess distribution to return of capital and capital gain distributions depends on the stock basis of the shareholder.

Question 3   MCQ-09632

On January 1, Year 5, Olinto Corp., an accrual-basis, calendar-year C corporation, had $35,000 in accumulated earnings and profits. For Year 5, Olinto had current earnings and profits of $15,000, and made two $40,000 cash distributions to its shareholders, one in April and one in September of Year 5. What amount of the Year 5 distributions is classified as dividend income to Olinto's shareholders?

1. $15,000
2. $35,000
3. $50,000
4. $80,000

© Becker Professional Education Corporation. All rights reserved.   *Regulation Final Review*   V   B-5

4 Corporate Distributions

4.1 Shareholder Taxable Amount

The taxable amount of a dividend from a corporation's earnings and profits depends upon the type of entity the shareholder is:

4.1.1 Individual Shareholder

- **Cash Dividends:** Amount received.
- **Property Dividends:** FMV of property received.

4.1.2 Corporate Shareholders

Remember the dividends received deduction.

- **Cash Dividends:** Amount received.
- **Property Dividends:** FMV of property received.

4.2 Corporation Paying Dividend—Taxable Amount

4.2.1 General Rule

The general rule is that the payment of a dividend does not create a taxable event. A dividend is a reduction of earnings and profits.

4.2.2 Property Dividends

If a corporation distributes appreciated property, the tax results are as follows:

- The corporation recognizes gain as if the property had been sold (i.e., FMV less adjusted basis). The gain increases current E&P.

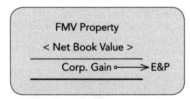

Question 4   MCQ-09619

Fox Corp. owned 2,000 shares of Duffy Corp., stock that it bought in Year 0 for $9 per share. In Year 8, when the fair market value of the Duffy stock was $20 per share, Fox distributed this stock to a noncorporate shareholder. Fox's recognized gain on this distribution was:

1. $40,000
2. $22,000
3. $18,000
4. $0

---

5 Corporate Liquidation

5.1 Corporation Sells Assets and Distributes Cash to Shareholders

▨ The corporation recognizes a gain or loss (as normal) on the sale of the assets; and

▨ Shareholders recognize gain or loss to the extent that cash differs from their adjusted basis of the stock.

5.2 Corporation Distributes Assets to Shareholders

▨ The corporation recognizes a gain or loss as if it sold the assets for FMV; and

▨ Shareholders recognize a gain or loss to the extent the FMV of the assets received differs from the adjusted basis of their stock.

Question 5   MCQ-09500

Krol Corp. distributed marketable securities in redemption of its stock in a complete liquidation. On the date of distribution, these securities had a basis of $100,000 and a fair market value of $150,000. What gain does Krol have as a result of the distribution?

1. $0.
2. $50,000 capital gain.
3. $50,000 Section 1231 gain.
4. $50,000 ordinary gain.

© Becker Professional Education Corporation. All rights reserved.   *Regulation Final Review*   **V   B-7**

Notes

1 S Corporation Eligibility

1.1 Eligible Shareholders

■ Eligible shareholders include individuals, estates, and certain types of trusts.

■ An individual shareholder may not be a nonresident alien.

■ Qualified retirement plans, trusts, and 501(c)(3) charitable organizations may be shareholders.

■ Neither corporations nor partnerships are eligible shareholders.

■ Grantor and voting trusts are permissible shareholders.

1.2 Shareholder Limit

There may not be more than 100 shareholders. Family members (current/ former spouses, common ancestors, and/or their descendants) may elect to be treated as one shareholder.

1.3 One Class of Stock

There may not be more than one class of stock outstanding. However, differences in common stock voting rights are allowed. Preferred stock is not permitted.

Question 1	MCQ-09531

Village Corp., a calendar year corporation, began business in Year 1. Village made a valid S corporation election on December 5, Year 4, with the unanimous consent of its shareholders. The eligibility requirements for S status continued to be met throughout Year 5. On what date did Village's S status become effective?

    1. January 1, Year 4.

    2. January 1, Year 5.

    3. December 5, Year 4.

    4. December 5, Year 5.

2 Effect of S Corporation Election

2.1 No Tax on Corporation

Generally, there is no tax at the corporation level. All earnings are passed through to the shareholders (i.e., the entity is taxed similar to a partnership); however, if the S corporation was previously a C corporation, there are three exceptions: LIFO recapture tax, built-in gains tax, and passive investment income tax.

2.2 Effect of S Corporation Election on Shareholders

2.2.1 Pass-Through of Income and/or Losses

Net income (or loss) is passed through to shareholders on Schedule K-1.

- The following S corporation items flow through to the shareholder in a manner similar to a partnership (see Schedule K-1 for a complete list):
  - Ordinary income (not subject to FICA)
  - Rental income/loss
  - Portfolio income (including interest, dividends, and royalties)
  - Tax-exempt interest
  - Capital gains and losses
  - Section 1231 gains and losses
  - Percentage depletion
  - Foreign income tax
  - Charitable contributions
  - Expense deduction for recovery property (Section 179)

- Allocations to shareholders are made on a per-share, per-day basis.
- Losses are limited to the shareholder's adjusted basis in the S corporation stock plus direct shareholder loans to the corporation.

2.2.2 Effect on Basis in S Corporation Stock

Income and capital contributions increase basis; losses and distributions decrease basis. Unlike partnership taxation, corporate debt does not increase a shareholder's basis in her or his stock of the S corporation.

Question 2   MCQ-09515

Fox Corp., an S corporation, had an ordinary loss of $36,500 for the year ended December 31, Year 2. At January 1, Year 2, Duffy owned 50% of Fox's stock. Duffy held the stock for 40 days in Year 2 before selling the entire 50% interest to an unrelated third party. Duffy's basis for the stock was $10,000. Duffy was a full-time employee of Fox until the stock was sold. Duffy's share of Fox's loss was:

1. $0
2. $2,000
3. $10,000
4. $18,250

3 Termination of S Election

The S corporation status will terminate as a result of any of the following:

■ A majority of the shareholders (any combination of voting and nonvoting) consent to a voluntary revocation.

■ The corporation fails to meet the criteria that allow S corporation status (e.g., the number of shareholders exceeds 100).

■ For each of three consecutive years, more than 25 percent of the corporation's gross receipts were from passive investment income and the corporation still had C corporation earnings and profits at the end of each year. In this case the S corporation status terminates at the beginning of the fourth year.

Question 3   MCQ-9452

An S Corporation has 30,000 shares of voting common stock and 20,000 shares of nonvoting common stock issued and outstanding. The S election can be revoked voluntarily with the consent of the shareholders holding, on the day of the revocation:

	Shares of Voting Stock	Shares of Nonvoting Stock
1.	0	20,000
2.	7,500	5,000
3.	10,000	16,000
4.	20,000	0

C   S Corporations

Task-Based Simulations

Task-Based Simulation: Research

What code section and subsection describes the eligibility criteria that must be met in order for a company to become a "small business corporation" (S corporation)?

Enter your response in the answer fields below. Guidance on correctly structuring your response appears above and below the answer fields.

> **Type the section here.**
> *Examples of correctly formatted sections are shown below.*

IRC § [   ] ([   ])

ⓘ Examples of correctly formatted IRC responses are IRC§1(a), IRC§56(a), IRC§54A(a), IRC§162(a), IRC§54AA(a), IRC§263a(a), IRC§1245(a), IRC§2032a(a), IRC§1400U-1(a).

Explanation

Source of answer for this question:

IRC Section 1361, Subsection (b)

Keywords: S corporation election

1 Basis

The general rule for taxable events and basis applies to partnership taxation as well as individual taxation:

Transactions				
Event		*Income*		*Basis*
Taxable	=	FMV	=	FMV
Nontaxable	=	N-O-N-E	=	NBV

1.1 Basis of Contributing Partner's Interest

1.1.1 Initial Basis

The partner's initial basis shall be the following:

- **Cash:** Amount contributed
- **Property:** Adjusted basis (NBV)
- **Liabilities:** Incoming partner's liabilities assumed by other partners is a reduction
- **Services:** Fair market value (and taxable to partner)
- **Liabilities:** Other partner's liabilities assumed by incoming partner

1.1.2 Property Subject to an Excess Liability

When property contributed by a partner is subject to a liability and the decrease in the partner's individual liability exceeds his or her partnership basis, the excess amount is not boot, but is treated like boot in that it generates a gain to the partner.

1.2 Partner Basis Formula

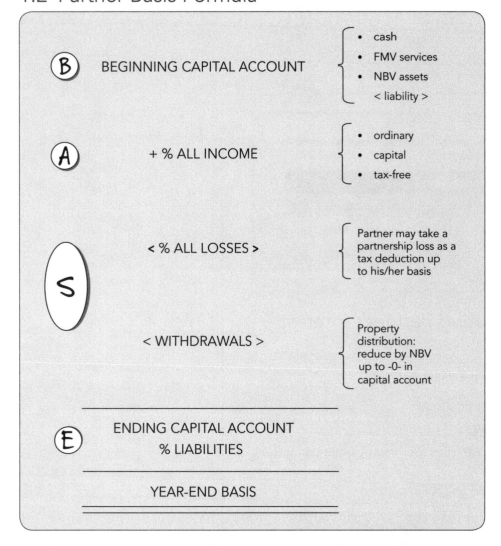

(B) BEGINNING CAPITAL ACCOUNT
- cash
- FMV services
- NBV assets
  < liability >

(A) + % ALL INCOME
- ordinary
- capital
- tax-free

(S)

< % ALL LOSSES >
Partner may take a partnership loss as a tax deduction up to his/her basis

< WITHDRAWALS >
Property distribution: reduce by NBV up to -0- in capital account

(E) ENDING CAPITAL ACCOUNT
% LIABILITIES

YEAR-END BASIS

Question 1   MCQ-09470

Gray is a 50% partner in Fabco Partnership. Gray's tax basis in Fabco on January 1, Year 4, was $5,000. Fabco made no distributions to the partners during Year 4, and recorded the following:

Ordinary income	$20,000
Tax exempt income	$ 8,000
Portfolio income	$ 4,000

What is Gray's tax basis in Fabco on December 31, Year 4?

1. $21,000
2. $16,000
3. $12,000
4. $10,000

2 Determination of Ordinary Income/ Loss and Separately Stated Items

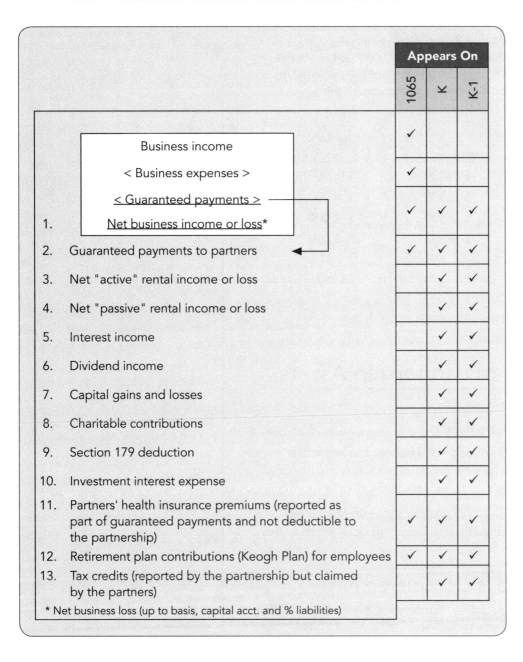

	Appears On		
	1065	K	K-1
Business income	✓		
< Business expenses >	✓		
< Guaranteed payments >	✓	✓	✓
1. Net business income or loss*			
2. Guaranteed payments to partners	✓	✓	✓
3. Net "active" rental income or loss		✓	✓
4. Net "passive" rental income or loss		✓	✓
5. Interest income		✓	✓
6. Dividend income		✓	✓
7. Capital gains and losses		✓	✓
8. Charitable contributions		✓	✓
9. Section 179 deduction		✓	✓
10. Investment interest expense		✓	✓
11. Partners' health insurance premiums (reported as part of guaranteed payments and not deductible to the partnership)	✓	✓	✓
12. Retirement plan contributions (Keogh Plan) for employees	✓	✓	✓
13. Tax credits (reported by the partnership but claimed by the partners)		✓	✓

* Net business loss (up to basis, capital acct. and % liabilities)

Question 2   MCQ-09652

Nick, Chris, Stacey, and Mike are each 25% partners in Liberty Partnership, a general partnership. During the current year, the partnership had revenues of $300,000 and non-separately allocated business expenses of $100,000, including a guaranteed payment of $30,000 to Nick for services rendered. Also, during the current year, the partnership had interest income of $10,000 and charitable contributions of $16,000. With regard to activity in the partnership, what should Stacey report on her income tax return for the current year?

	Ordinary Income	Interest Income	Charitable Contributions
1.	$200,000	$10,000	$16,000
2.	$ 80,000	$ 2,500	$ 4,000
3.	$ 57,500	$ 2,500	$ 4,000
4.	$ 50,000	$ 2,500	$ 4,000

3 Distribution of Partnership Assets

3.1 General (Nontaxable)

In general, a nonliquidating distribution to a partner is nontaxable.

3.2 Basis Reduction

In general, distributions of cash or property to a partner reduce the partner's basis by the cash or the adjusted basis (net book value) of the property distributed.

3.3 Cash Received Is Considered First

In both nonliquidating and liquidating distributions, the cash received in the transaction is applied first as a reduction of the partner's basis in the partnership before any property distributions are considered.

3.4 Property – NBV

In a nonliquidating distribution, the basis of property received by the partner will be the same as the basis in the hands of the partnership immediately prior to the distribution.

3.5 Reduction (for a Withdrawal) Limited to Partnership Basis

■ The assigned basis of the property received may not exceed the partner's basis in the partnership. Cash received is applied first.

■ If the amount of cash received exceeds the partner's basis in the partnership, gain is recognized to the extent of the excess. Any property received in the same transaction would have a basis to the partner of zero.

■ If cash received is less than the partner's basis in the partnership, but application of the general rule (in the item above) would cause the basis of the partnership to go below zero, basis is allocated to the property in the amount that would reduce the partner's basis in the partnership to zero.

Question 3   MCQ-09485

Day's adjusted basis in LMN Partnership interest is $50,000. During the year Day received a nonliquidating distribution of $25,000 cash plus land with an adjusted basis of $15,000 to LMN, and a fair market value of $20,000. How much is Day's basis in the land?

1. $10,000
2. $15,000
3. $20,000
4. $25,000

4 Ownership Changes and Liquidation

4.1 Complete Withdrawal (Liquidation)

In a complete liquidation, the partner's basis for the distributed property is the same as the adjusted basis of his partnership interest, reduced by any cash received in the same transaction.

4.1.1 Nontaxable Liquidation

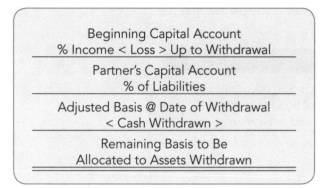

Beginning Capital Account
% Income < Loss > Up to Withdrawal

Partner's Capital Account
% of Liabilities

Adjusted Basis @ Date of Withdrawal
< Cash Withdrawn >

Remaining Basis to Be
Allocated to Assets Withdrawn

The CPA Examination will require candidates to understand the difference in basis rules for nonliquidating and liquidating distributions.

Withdrawal	Basis Used	Stopping Point
Nonliquidating	NBV Asset Taken	Stop at Zero
Liquidating	Partnership Interest	Must "Zero Out" Account

4.2 Sale of Partnership Interest

As a general rule, the partner has a capital gain or loss when transferring a partnership interest because a partnership interest is a capital asset.

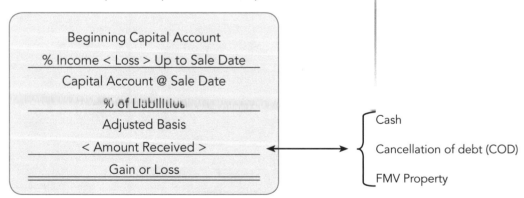

Beginning Capital Account
% Income < Loss > Up to Sale Date

Capital Account @ Sale Date
% of Liabilities

Adjusted Basis
< Amount Received >

Gain or Loss

- Cash
- Cancellation of debt (COD)
- FMV Property

Question 4

MCQ-09581

On December 31 of the current year, after receipt of his share of partnership income, Fox sold his interest in a limited partnership for $50,000 cash and relief of all liabilities. On that date, the adjusted basis of Fox's partnership interest was $60,000 consisting of his capital account of $35,000 and his share of the partnership liabilities of $25,000. The partnership has no unrealized receivables or substantially appreciated inventory. What is Fox's gain or loss on the sale of his partnership interest?

1. Ordinary loss of $10,000
2. Ordinary gain of $15,000
3. Capital loss of $10,000
4. Capital gain of $15,000

D   Partnerships

Task-Based Simulations

Task-Based Simulation 1: Partnership Tax Return

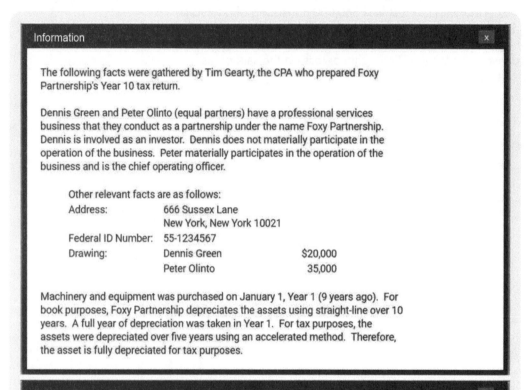

Information

The following facts were gathered by Tim Gearty, the CPA who prepared Foxy Partnership's Year 10 tax return.

Dennis Green and Peter Olinto (equal partners) have a professional services business that they conduct as a partnership under the name Foxy Partnership. Dennis is involved as an investor. Dennis does not materially participate in the operation of the business. Peter materially participates in the operation of the business and is the chief operating officer.

Other relevant facts are as follows:

Address:	666 Sussex Lane	
	New York, New York 10021	
Federal ID Number:	55-1234567	
Drawing:	Dennis Green	$20,000
	Peter Olinto	35,000

Machinery and equipment was purchased on January 1, Year 1 (9 years ago). For book purposes, Foxy Partnership depreciates the assets using straight-line over 10 years. A full year of depreciation was taken in Year 1. For tax purposes, the assets were depreciated over five years using an accelerated method. Therefore, the asset is fully depreciated for tax purposes.

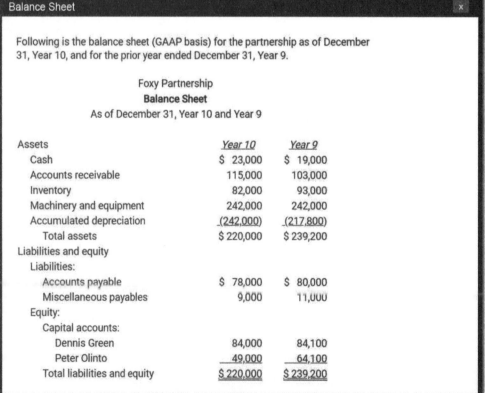

Balance Sheet

Following is the balance sheet (GAAP basis) for the partnership as of December 31, Year 10, and for the prior year ended December 31, Year 9.

Foxy Partnership
Balance Sheet
As of December 31, Year 10 and Year 9

Assets	Year 10	Year 9
Cash	$ 23,000	$ 19,000
Accounts receivable	115,000	103,000
Inventory	82,000	93,000
Machinery and equipment	242,000	242,000
Accumulated depreciation	(242,000)	(217,800)
Total assets	$ 220,000	$ 239,200
Liabilities and equity		
Liabilities:		
Accounts payable	$ 78,000	$ 80,000
Miscellaneous payables	9,000	11,000
Equity:		
Capital accounts:		
Dennis Green	84,000	84,100
Peter Olinto	49,000	64,100
Total liabilities and equity	$ 220,000	$ 239,200

Income Statement   x

Following is the Income Statement for the current year, Year 10.

Foxy Partnership
Income Statement
For the Year Ended December 31, Year 10

Revenues	Book Income
Sales	$925,000
Dividends (Qualified)	1,600
Interest	3,200
Total revenue	$929,800
Cost of goods sold	555,000
Gross profit	374,800
Expenses	
Guaranteed payments to partners:	
Dennis Green	0
Peter Olinto	25,000
Salaries and wages	209,000
Depreciation	24,200
Insurance	42,000
Business meals	2,000
Rent	12,000
Repairs and maintenance	15,000
Charitable contributions	4,000
Total expenses	333,200
Net income	$ 41,600

D Partnerships

Scroll down to complete all parts of this task.

Using the information contained in the exhibits, enter the appropriate amounts to be reported on Foxy Partnership's partnership tax return. Enter all amounts as positive whole numbers. If a response is zero, enter a zero (0).

	A	B
1	Gross receipts or sales	123
2	Cost of goods sold	123
3	Salaries and wages	123
4	Guaranteed payments to partners	123
5	Repairs and maintenance	123
6	Bad debts	123
7	Rent	123
8	Depreciation	123
9	Other deductions	123
10	Ordinary business income (loss)	123

Explanation

Gross receipts or sales:	$925,000	
Cost of goods sold:	$555,000	
Salaries and wages:	$209,000	
Guaranteed payments to partners:	$25,000	
Repairs and maintenance:	$15,000	
Bad debts:	0	There is no bad debt
Rent:	$12,000	
Depreciation:	$0	Although still depreciating for GAAP, fully depreciated for tax purposes
Other deductions:	$43,000	(Insurance $42,000 + 50% of business meals $1,000)
Ordinary business income (loss):	$66,000	This is the gross receipts less all of the deductions listed.

D Partnerships

Task-Based Simulation 2: Partnership Schedule K

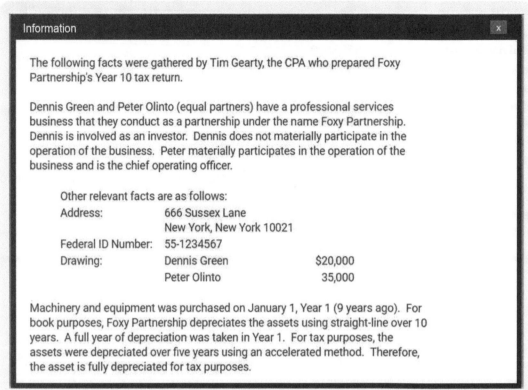

Information

The following facts were gathered by Tim Gearty, the CPA who prepared Foxy Partnership's Year 10 tax return.

Dennis Green and Peter Olinto (equal partners) have a professional services business that they conduct as a partnership under the name Foxy Partnership. Dennis is involved as an investor. Dennis does not materially participate in the operation of the business. Peter materially participates in the operation of the business and is the chief operating officer.

Other relevant facts are as follows:

Address:	666 Sussex Lane	
	New York, New York 10021	
Federal ID Number:	55-1234567	
Drawing:	Dennis Green	$20,000
	Peter Olinto	35,000

Machinery and equipment was purchased on January 1, Year 1 (9 years ago). For book purposes, Foxy Partnership depreciates the assets using straight-line over 10 years. A full year of depreciation was taken in Year 1. For tax purposes, the assets were depreciated over five years using an accelerated method. Therefore, the asset is fully depreciated for tax purposes.

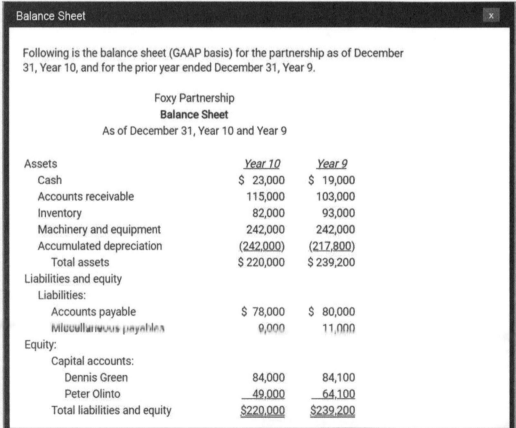

Balance Sheet

Following is the balance sheet (GAAP basis) for the partnership as of December 31, Year 10, and for the prior year ended December 31, Year 9.

Foxy Partnership
Balance Sheet
As of December 31, Year 10 and Year 9

Assets	Year 10	Year 9
Cash	$ 23,000	$ 19,000
Accounts receivable	115,000	103,000
Inventory	82,000	93,000
Machinery and equipment	242,000	242,000
Accumulated depreciation	(242,000)	(217,800)
Total assets	$ 220,000	$ 239,200
Liabilities and equity		
Liabilities:		
Accounts payable	$ 78,000	$ 80,000
Miscellaneous payables	9,000	11,000
Equity:		
Capital accounts:		
Dennis Green	84,000	84,100
Peter Olinto	49,000	64,100
Total liabilities and equity	$220,000	$239,200

Income Statement   x

Following is the Income Statement for the current year, Year 10.

Foxy Partnership
Income Statement
For the Year Ended December 31, Year 10

Revenues	Book Income
Sales	$925,000
Dividends (Qualified)	1,600
Interest	3,200
Total revenue	$929,800
Cost of goods sold	555,000
Gross profit	374,800
Expenses	
Guaranteed payments to partners:	
Dennis Green	0
Peter Olinto	25,000
Salaries and wages	209,000
Depreciation	24,200
Insurance	42,000
Business meals	2,000
Rent	12,000
Repairs and maintenance	15,000
Charitable contributions	4,000
Total expenses	333,200
Net income	$ 41,600

D   Partnerships

EXHIBITS   close all exhibits

📄 Information   📄 Balance Sheet   📄 Income Statement

Scroll down to complete all parts of this task.

Enter the appropriate amounts to be reported on Foxy Partnership's Schedule K.

	A	B
1	Ordinary income (loss) from trade or business activities	123
2	Interest income	123
3	Dividends	123
4	Other portfolio income (loss)	123
5	Guaranteed payments to partners	123
6	Charitable contributions	123
7	Section 179 expense deduction	123
8	Nondeductible expenses	123
9	Distributions of cash	123

Explanation

Ordinary income (loss) from trade or business activities:	$66,000	Ordinary business income from Form 1065 *(925,000 - 555,000 - 25,000 - 209,000 - 42,000 - 1,000 - 12,000 - 15,000 = 66,000)*
Interest income:	$3,200	Given
Dividends:	$1,600	Given
Other portfolio income (loss):	$0	N/A
Guaranteed payments to partners:	$25,000	Given
Charitable contributions:	$4,000	Given
Section 179 deduction:	$0	N/A
Nondeductible expenses:	$1,000	50% nondeductible portion of business meals
Distributions of cash:	$55,000	This is the total of the two partners' cash withdrawals

D Partnerships

Task-Based Simulation 3: Partnership Non-liquidating Distribution

Scroll down to complete all parts of this task.

Gearty's basis in his ABC partnership interest before any partnership distributions is $50,000. In a non-liquidating distribution, the partnership distributed to Gearty cash of $20,000, business-use property with a fair market value of $60,000, and a basis in the hands of the partnership of $25,000.

Answer the questions related to Gearty's non-liquidating partnership distribution in the table below. Enter all amounts as positive whole numbers. If the response is zero, enter a zero (0).

	A	B
1	What amount of taxable income does Gearty recognize related to the distribution?	[123]
2	What is Gearty's basis in his partnership interest after the distribution?	[123]
3	What is Gearty's basis in the property received from the partnership?	[123]

Explanation

Row 1: $0

Row 2: $5,000

Row 3: $25,000

A non-liquidating distribution of cash will reduce the partner's basis in his partnership interest by the amount of cash distributed. Such distribution is a non-taxable event to the partner, provided the cash distribution is not greater than the partner's basis in his partnership interest prior to distribution. If the cash distributed is greater than the partner's basis in his partnership interest prior to the distribution, such excess cash distributed is a taxable gain to the partner.

A non-liquidating distribution of property will reduce the partner's basis in his partnership interest by the amount of the partnership's basis in the property. The partner's basis in the property received will be the same as the basis in the hands of the partnership, limited to the partner's basis in his partnership interest.

If both cash and property are distributed, cash reduces the partner's basis in the partnership interest first, then property.

Basis in partnership interest before distributions	$ 50,000
Cash distribution	(20,000)
Basis in partnership interest after cash distribution	$ 30,000
Distribution of property with basis of $25,000	(25,000)
Basis in partnership interest after distributions	$ 5,000

Gearty's basis in his partnership interest is reduced to $5,000 after the distributions.

Gearty's basis in the property received is $25,000, which is the partnership's basis in the property.

Notes

1 Distributable Net Income

Distributable net income (DNI) is a limitation on the amount the trust or estate can deduct (on line 18 of IRS Form 1041) with respect to distributions to beneficiaries. Set forth below is the general calculation of DNI:

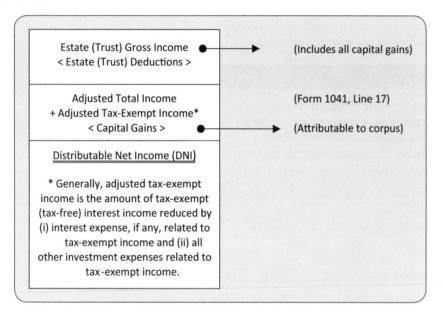

Estate (Trust) Gross Income < Estate (Trust) Deductions >	(Includes all capital gains)
Adjusted Total Income + Adjusted Tax-Exempt Income* < Capital Gains >	(Form 1041, Line 17) (Attributable to corpus)

Distributable Net Income (DNI)

* Generally, adjusted tax-exempt income is the amount of tax-exempt (tax-free) interest income reduced by (i) interest expense, if any, related to tax-exempt income and (ii) all other investment expenses related to tax-exempt income.

1.1 Gross Income

Gross income is generally determined in the same manner as it is for individuals. Gross income includes capital gains.

1.2 Deductions

Deductions are allowed for ordinary and necessary expenses incurred for any of the following:

- Carrying on a trade or business.
- Production of income.
- Management or conservation of income-producing property.
- Determination, collection, or refund of any tax.
- Contributions to a charity (an unlimited charitable deduction is allowed if the will or trust document provides for such contributions).

1.3 Tax-Exempt Income

Although it is not subject to income tax, tax-exempt income is included in DNI.

1.4 Capital Gains

Capital gains are attributable to corpus and are generally not included in DNI. Therefore, they must be deducted from the gross income of the trust or estate to arrive at DNI, unless it specifically indicates differently in the facts.

1.5 Income Distribution Deduction

The income distribution deduction reduces the taxable income of the trust or estate. The income distribution deduction equals the lesser of:

- DNI (less adjusted tax-exempt income); or
- Total distributions (including income required to be distributed currently) reduced by tax-exempt income (not adjusted tax-exempt income).

Question 1   MCQ-09455

Lyon, a cash basis taxpayer, died on January 15 of the current year. During the current year, the estate executor made the required periodic distribution of $9,000 from estate income to Lyon's sole heir. The following pertains to the estate's income and disbursements for the year:

Estate Income	
$20,000	Taxable interest
$10,000	Net long-term capital gains allocable to corpus

Estate Disbursements	
$5,000	Administrative expenses attributable to taxable income

For the current calendar year, what was the estate's distributable net income (DNI)?

1. $15,000
2. $20,000
3. $25,000
4. $30,000

---

2 Form 1041—Estates and Trusts

2.1 Annual Trust Income Tax Return

Trusts are subject only to income tax and are considered separate tax paying entities. Trusts are classified as either simple or complex.

2.1.1 Year-End—Calendar

All trusts (except tax-exempt trusts such as a pension plan trust) must use a calendar year.

2.1.2 Distributable Net Income

Trust may deduct amounts distributed to beneficiaries up to the amount of DNI less adjusted tax-exempt income (as shown above).

2.1.3 Simple Trusts

- A simple trust only makes distributions out of current income (i.e., it cannot make distributions from the trust corpus).
- A simple trust is required to distribute all of its income currently.
- A simple trust cannot take a deduction for a charitable contribution.
- A simple trust is entitled to a $300 exemption in arriving at its taxable income.

2.1.4 Complex Trusts

All trusts that are not simple trusts are complex trusts. A trust may be simple one year and complex the next.

- A complex trust may accumulate current income.
- A complex trust may distribute principal.
- A complex trust may provide for charitable contributions.
- A complex trust is permitted an exemption of $100 in arriving at its taxable income.

2.1.5 Grantor Trusts

In a grantor trust, the grantor (the individual who established the trust) retains control over the trust assets. A grantor trust is considered a disregarded entity for income tax purposes. Any taxable income or deduction of a grantor trust is reported on the income tax return of the grantor.

2.1.6 Due Date for Filing

The due date for filing a trust's Form 1041 is April 15th, but an extension to file is available.

2.2 Annual Estate Income Tax Return

Estates are taxable entities that come into existence upon the death of an individual and continue to exist until all assets of the estate are distributed. The calculation for the taxable income of an estate is similar to that of trusts. However, the following items differ:

- Estate exemption: $600.

- Estate year-end: calendar or fiscal.

- Filing due date: 15th day of the fourth month following the end of the tax year.

Question 2   MCQ-09610

Lyon, a cash basis taxpayer, died on January 15 of the current year. During the current year, the estate executor made the required periodic distribution of $9,000 from estate income to Lyon's sole heir. The following pertains to the estate's income and disbursements for the current year:

Estate Income

$20,000	Taxable interest
$10,000	Net long-term capital gains allocable to corpus

Estate Disbursements

$5,000	Administrative expenses attributable to taxable income

Lyon's executor does not intend to file an extension request for the estate fiduciary income tax return. By what date must the executor file the Form 1041, U.S. Fiduciary Income Tax Return, for the estate's current calendar year?

1. March 15 of the following year
2. April 15 of the following year
3. June 15 of the following year
4. September 15 of the following year

---

1 Types of Exempt Organizations

1.1 Section 501(c)(1) Corporations

- Section 501(c)(1) corporations are created by an act of Congress.

- Almost all other exempt organizations must make written application for exempt status, be approved by the IRS, become incorporated, and issue capital stock. Furthermore, the articles of organization must limit the purpose of the entity to the charitable/exempt purpose.

1.2 Section 501(c)(2) Corporations

Organized for an exclusive purpose to hold title to property, collect income from the property, and turn over the net income to an exempt organization.

1.3 Section 501(c)(3) Corporations

Will lose tax-exempt status if any one or more of the following situations occur:

- Any part of the earnings inure to the benefit of a private shareholder or individual.

- A substantial part of the activities are nonexempt activities (e.g., carrying on propaganda or attempting to influence legislation).

- The organization directly participates or intervenes in a political campaign.

1.4 Section 509 Private Foundations

- **General Rules:** These include all 501(c)(3) corporations except (1) maximum (60-percent-type) charitable deduction donees; (2) broadly publicly supported organizations receiving more than 1/3 of their annual support from members and the public and less than 1/3 from investment income and unrelated business income; (3) supporting organizations; and (4) public safety testing organizations.

- **Termination:** This can be involuntary (e.g., when private corporations become public charities) or voluntary (private foundation status need not be permanent and termination may be achieved by notifying the IRS).

2 Unrelated Business Income (UBI)

2.1 Definition

Unrelated business income (UBI) is the gross income from any unrelated trade or business "regularly" carried on, minus business deductions directly connected therewith. UBI is:

- derived from an activity that constitutes a trade or business;
- regularly carried on; and
- not substantially related to the organization's tax-exempt purposes.

2.2 Taxation of UBI

Although an organization may have tax-exempt status, the organization may become subject to regular corporate income tax on income from a business enterprise that is not related to its tax-exempt purpose (UBI).

- **$1,000 Specific Deduction:** Only UBI in excess of $1,000 is subject to tax.
- **Excluded Items of Income:** Certain types of "unrelated" income are excluded from tax (e.g., income from research of a college or hospital; activities limited to exempt organizations by state law; royalties, dividends, interest, and most annuities; gains and losses on the sale or exchange of property not held primarily for sale to customers in the ordinary course of trade or business; and income from the exchange or rental of membership lists of tax-exempt charitable organizations).

2.3 Membership Organizations

If a social club makes a profit, that profit is generally taxable.

2.4 "Feeder Organizations"

An organization that is operated primarily for the purpose of carrying on a trade or business for profit cannot claim exemption from tax on the grounds that all of its profits are payable to tax-exempt organizations.

Note

The CPA Exam will attempt to confuse the candidate by asking questions regarding "unrelated" activities. Be aware that an unrelated business does not include any activity where all of the work is performed by unpaid workers (volunteers); thus, an organization's use of unpaid workers makes the business or activity "related" and not taxable. Furthermore, sales of articles made by disabled persons as part of their rehabilitation are deemed "related" and are not taxable.

Note

The fact that an activity results in a loss does not exclude that activity from the definition of an unrelated business (if expenses exceed income, a net operating loss exists, which is subject to carryover provisions of net operating losses).

Question 1   MCQ-09657

Unrelated business income (UBI):

1. Includes unrelated income from an activity where all the work is performed by volunteers.
2. Does not apply if the activity results in a loss.
3. Is 100% taxable on the exempt organization's tax return.
4. Specifically excludes income from the research of a college or hospital.

3 Annual Return Requirement

3.1 General

An annual information return (Form 990) stating gross income, receipts, contributions, disbursements, etc., is required of most organizations exempt from tax under Code Section 501 and is open to public inspection.

3.2 Exceptions

There are three types of exempt organizations that do not have an annual filing requirement of a Form 990/990-EZ information return with the IRS:

■ **Religious Organizations:** Churches and exclusively religious activities of a religious order or internally supported auxiliaries.

■ **Certain Organizations That Normally Have Less Than $5,000 in Annual Gross Receipts:** These organizations include educational organizations, religious organizations, public-type charities, fraternal organizations, and those organized to prevent cruelty to children or animals. A simple electronic postcard (Form 990-N) is required to be filed, however.

■ **Organizations That Normally Have Less Than $50,000 in Annual Gross Receipts:** If an organization has gross receipts of less than $50,000 (years 2010 and later), a Form 990 or 990-EZ is not required to be filed. A simple electronic "postcard" (Form 990-N) is filed with the IRS and requires only the following information: (1) the tax identification number of the organization; (2) the tax year of the organization; (3) the legal name, physical address, and internet address (if applicable) of the organization; (4) the name and address of the principal officer of the organization; and (5) a statement that the annual gross receipts of the organization regularly do not exceed the $50,000 limit.

3.3 Penalties

Penalties apply for failure to file a required tax form (including the 990-N) and failing to comply with the requirements and disclosures of the exempt organization. Furthermore, if an organization fails to file the required return for three consecutive years, the tax-exempt status of the organization will be revoked.

Question 2   MCQ-09658

Which of the following is a false statement?

1. An annual information return (Form 990) stating gross income, receipts, contributions, and disbursements is required of most exempt organizations that are exempt from tax.

2. For organizations that normally have less than $50,000 in annual gross receipts, a Form 990 or 990-EZ is not required; however, an electronic postcard (Form 990-N) is filed with the IRS and provides only limited information.

3. An organization operated primarily for the purposes of carrying on a trade or business for profit is able to claim exemption from tax if all of its profits are payable to exempt organizations.

4. If an organization fails to file the required return for three consecutive years, the tax-exempt status of the organization will be revoked.

Class Question Explanations

Regulation Final Review

Topic A

QUESTION 1   MCQ-09715

Choice "4" is correct.

Practitioners must apply due diligence standards to all written advice, including those by means of electronic communication, regarding one or more federal tax matters.

Choice "1" is incorrect. Prior to June 12, 2014, a different set of provisions applied to advice that was defined as a "covered" opinion.

Choice "2" is incorrect. The provisions in effect prior to June 12, 2014, excluded certain written opinions.

Choice "3" is incorrect. The requirements of Circular 230 apply to all applicable written advice, regardless of the principal purpose of the entity or plan.

QUESTION 2   MCQ-09712

Choice "4" is correct.

A compensated preparer is liable for a penalty if the preparer's understatement of taxpayer liability on a return or claim for refund is due to the preparer's negligent or intentional disregard of rules and regulations. In this situation, Mr. Powell knew that the income earned as an independent contractor by the taxpayer should be reported on the taxpayer's income tax return; however, he intentionally disregarded the rules associated with the reporting of this income.

Choice "1" is incorrect. Substantial authority refers to a standard that is used in determining whether or not a tax position taken in a tax return is supported by relevant tax authorities. A tax return preparer who takes an unreasonable position in a tax return that is not supported by substantial authority may be liable for the penalty associated with the understatement of the taxpayer's liability due to an *unreasonable position* by the *tax return preparer.*

Choice "2" is incorrect. Failure to file correct information returns refers to the penalty assessed on a person who employs a tax return preparer and fails to file an information return containing the name, taxpayer identification number, and place of work of each tax return preparer.

Choice "3" is incorrect. Wrongful disclosure and/or use of tax return information by the tax return preparer refers to the penalty imposed on a tax return preparer for wrongfully disclosing information provided by the taxpayer.

Regulation I

Topic B

QUESTION 1   MCQ-09719

Choice "3" is correct.

The U.S. Tax Court is the only forum in which taxpayers may litigate without first having to pay the disputed tax in full.

Choice "1" is incorrect. A case would not start in the U.S. Supreme Court. The U.S. Supreme Court only rarely hears tax cases. When a case makes it to the Supreme Court, it is typically when where there is a conflict among the Courts of Appeals or a tax issue of major importance.

Choice "2" is incorrect. A taxpayer who disagrees with the IRS may take his or her case to a U.S. District Court only after paying the disputed tax liability and then sue the IRS/government for a refund.

Choice "4" is incorrect. To start the litigation process in the U.S. Court of Federal Claims, the taxpayer must pay the disputed tax and sue the IRS/government for a refund.

QUESTION 2   MCQ-09705

Choice "2" is correct.

The failure-to-pay penalty will apply to Spayer, and the failure-to-pay penalty is generally 0.5% of the tax due for each month (or any fraction thereof) the tax is not paid, up to a maximum of 25% of the unpaid tax.

Choice "1" is incorrect. The failure-to-file penalty will apply to Spayer, but the failure-to-file penalty is generally 5%, not 10%, of the tax due for each month (or any fraction thereof), not year, the return is not filed, up to a maximum of 25% of the unpaid tax.

Choice "3" is incorrect. If both the failure-to-file penalty and the failure-to-pay penalty apply, the failure-to-file penalty is reduced by the amount of the failure-to-pay penalty. The penalty is thus not the total of the two penalties.

Choice "4" is incorrect. The penalty for failure to file a partnership tax return is $200 for each month or part thereof (up to a maximum of twelve months) the return is late (or required information is missing) times the number of persons who are partners in the partnership at any time during the year.

Topic C

QUESTION 1   MCQ-09540

Choice "2" is correct.

A client can recover from a CPA for negligence, gross negligence, or fraud. Negligence requires proof of the least culpable conduct, a failure to exercise due care.

Choice "1" is incorrect. Gross negligence (constructive fraud) occurs when an accountant, because of a reckless disregard for the truth, either makes a misrepresentation of a material fact or omits a material fact. Proving that Johnson acted recklessly would be more difficult than proving that Johnson failed to use reasonable care. Or, to put it simply, gross negligence requires a greater degree of culpability than ordinary negligence.

Choice "3" is incorrect. Fraud is an intentional tort. Rhodes would have to prove that Johnson acted with scienter. This would require proof that Johnson knowingly or intentionally failed to disclose the liability. Johnson could be liable for ordinary negligence even if it was unaware of the liability.

Choice "4" is incorrect. Johnson could be liable for ordinary negligence even if it was unaware of the liability. Failure to exercise due care requires proof of conduct less culpable than knowledge.

QUESTION 2   MCQ-09572

Choice "2" is correct.

Fraud has five elements: either a misrepresentation of a material fact or an omission of a material fact; scienter (intent to deceive or reckless disregard for the truth); reliance; intent to induce reliance; and damages. There can be no fraud if the false statements were immaterial.

Choice "1" is incorrect because lack of privity is only a defense to negligence. It is not a defense to fraud.

Choice "3" is incorrect. Whether or not the CPA financially benefited from the fraud is irrelevant.

Choice "4" is incorrect. Contributory negligence is only a defense to negligence. It is not a defense to fraud.

QUESTION 3   MCQ-09492

Choice "2" is correct.

Confidential client information may be revealed to a state CPA society voluntary quality control review board without the client's permission.

Choice "1" is incorrect because confidential client information may be revealed to others with the consent of the client. Thus, it can be waived by the client.

Choice "3" is incorrect. All states recognize the attorney-client privilege. Not all states recognize the accountant-client privilege.

Choice "4" is incorrect. The accountant-client privilege applies to oral and written communications.

Regulation Final Review

Topic A

QUESTION 1

Choice "4" is correct.

If an agent has paid for the right to be appointed as an agent, the agency is coupled with an interest and may be revoked only by the agent. The principal may not terminate the agency, and the agency does not terminate by operation of law by the death of the principal.

Choices "1", "2", and "3" are incorrect, per the above explanation.

QUESTION 2

Choice "4" is correct.

If the principal fires an agent, the principal must give actual notice to persons with whom the agent has dealt and constructive notice to all others. Failure to give the required notice leaves the agent with apparent authority to act on behalf of the principal.

Choices "1", "2", and "3" are incorrect. An agency terminated by law ends automatically without notice to any party. Agencies are terminated by law by death or insanity of either party, by bankruptcy of the principal, or by failure of the agent to have a required license and by destruction of a subject essential to the agency.

QUESTION 3

Choice "4" is correct.

To ratify a contract, the principal must have knowledge of all material facts.

Choice "1" is incorrect. Ratification does not require notification to be effective (the third party already thinks he or she has a contract with the principal).

Choice "2" is incorrect. If the principal ratifies an unauthorized contract, the principal is bound even if the agent acted unreasonably.

Choice "3" is incorrect. There is no requirement that an agent be a general agent in order to give a principal the right to ratify; principals may ratify contracts of special agents as well. It may even be possible to ratify a contract entered into by someone who was not an agent of the principal but purported to be one.

QUESTION 4

Choice "4" is correct.

Generally, a principal is not liable for an agent's torts. However, an employer is liable for an employee's torts committed within the scope of the employment (i.e., while the employee was attending to the employer's business). Here, Ed completed the requested delivery and then continued 10 miles out of his way to get to his mother's house where the collision occurred. Thus, the collision occurred outside of the scope of the employment and Phil will not be held liable.

Choice "1" is incorrect because it is not enough merely that Ed was Phil's employee; the tort must also occur within the scope of the employment. As explained above, the collision here did not occur within the scope of Ed's employment. He was on a frolic of his own.

Choice "2" is incorrect. It is not enough merely that Ed was driving Phil's truck. Ed must be an employee and the tort must have been committed within the scope of the employment. See above.

Choice "3" is incorrect. It is not enough merely that Ed was negligent. Ed must be an employee and the tort must have been committed within the scope of the employment. See above.

Regulation II

Topic B

QUESTION 1   MCQ-09456

Choice "2" is correct.

Most offers can be revoked anytime prior to acceptance. This is true even if the offer states it will be held open.

Choice "1" is incorrect because an option contract requires consideration to support the promise to keep the offer open and none was given here.

Choices "3" and "4" are incorrect because the firm offer rule applies only to the sale of goods by a merchant, not to the sale of real estate.

QUESTION 2   MCQ-09520

Choice "4" is correct.

The statute of limitations bars access to court remedies if suit is not brought within 4 to 6 years (in most states) after the date of the breach.

Choice "1" is incorrect because the time period varies from state to state. Four, five or six years is typical.

Choice "2" is incorrect because recording of the contract will have no effect on the contract.

Choice "3" is incorrect because the time period is measured from the date of the breach, not from when the contract is recorded.

QUESTION 3   MCQ-09612

Choice "4" is correct.

Specific performance is a court order requiring the breaching party to perform as promised under a contract. A court will not order a person to perform a non-assignable duty, as such an order would constitute involuntary servitude. The duties of a CPA are not assignable because they rely on the skills of the particular CPA.

Choices "1" and "3" are incorrect. By breaching the contract prior to the date of performance, Lark committed an anticipatory repudiation. An anticipatory repudiation permits Bale, the injured party, to sue Lark immediately or wait until the time of performance has passed and then sue.

Choice "2" is incorrect. Anytime there is a breach of contract, the injured party has the right to sue for compensatory damages and receive an award of money to compensate for all harm done.

QUESTION 4   MCQ-09505

Choice "4" is correct.

The statute of frauds requires a writing for most contracts for the sale of goods of $500 or more. A writing is not required, however, if the party admits in court that he made the contract.

Choices "1" and "2" are incorrect because part performance of a contract within the statute of frauds makes the contract enforceable only to the extent of the performance tendered and accepted. This question required the contract to be enforced in its entirety.

Choice "3" is incorrect because the contract involved the sale of goods of $500 or more.

QUESTION 5 MCQ-09489

Choice "2" is correct.

A buyer may reject any nonconforming delivery made by a seller. The seller has the right to correct or cure the nonconforming delivery by notifying the buyer it will be corrected on time. Thus, Kirk may deliver the freezer on June 23 by notifying Nix of its intent to do so.

Choice "1" is incorrect because notice is required to cure.

Choice "3" is incorrect because a buyer has an absolute right to reject a nonconforming delivery.

Choice "4" is incorrect because a seller has the right to cure or correct nonconforming deliveries if time is left before performance is due under the contract.

Topic C

QUESTION 1 MCQ-09587

Choice "2" is correct.

Contribution (a right to a pro rata payment of monies owed to a creditor) is a right a surety has against a cosurety.

Choices "1", "3", and "4" are incorrect. All three are available to a surety against the principal. Exoneration is the right to compel the principal to pay. Subrogation is the surety's right to succeed to the creditor's rights against the principal debtor after the surety pays the creditor. Reimbursement is the surety's right to recover from the principal whatever the surety pays the creditor.

QUESTION 2 MCQ-09560

Choice "4" is correct.

A transfer of property (including cash) from a debtor to a creditor made on account of an antecedent debt while the debtor was insolvent and within 90 days of the filing of a bankruptcy petition (one year for insiders) that allows the creditor to receive more than he would have received in a bankruptcy distribution is a preferential transfer that can be set aside by the trustee in bankruptcy. The $700 payment here was on account of an antecedent debt and meets the other requirements.

Choice "1" is incorrect. The $700 donation was not made on account of an antecedent debt, but rather was a gift. It might be set aside as a fraudulent transfer, but it does not qualify as a preference.

Choice "2" is incorrect. Because the utility bill is current, this is treated as a contemporaneous exchange for new value rather than an antecedent debt and does not qualify as a preference.

Choice "3" is incorrect. Because the payment was made to a fully secured creditor, the creditor did not get anything more than he would have received anyway (secured creditors are paid first and the facts say that the creditor was fully secured). Thus, the payment is not a preference.

QUESTION 3 MCQ-09576

Choice "3" is correct.

A debtor must wait at least eight years before receiving another discharge.

Choices "1", "2", and "4" are incorrect. They all are examples of specific debts that will not be discharged, but the mere fact that such debts are owed is not a ground for denying a discharge for a petitioner's other debts.

Regulation II

QUESTION 4

Choice "4" is correct.

A purchase money security interest (PMSI) in equipment is superior to almost any other interest a third party might have in the same item of collateral if the security interest is perfected within 20 days after the debtor obtains possession of the collateral. A PMSI arises when a creditor either (i) lends the debtor the money that was used to purchase the collateral; or (ii) sells the collateral to the debtor on credit and retains a security interest for the purchase price. Here, the creditor lent the debtor the money that the debtor used to buy the equipment, and the lender perfected by filing on January 30, which is within 20 days after the debtor received possession of the equipment on January 20. Thus, the creditor here has a perfected PMSI which is superior to most other interests in the same item of collateral.

Choice "1" is incorrect. Although the general rule is that when creditors have conflicting perfected security interests in the same item of collateral, the first to file or perfect has priority, and the creditor here filed before the creditor in choice "4" filed or perfected, a properly perfected PMSI takes priority. Thus, the creditor in choice "1" is subordinate to the creditor in choice "4".

Choice "2" is incorrect. Taking possession of collateral to perfect a security interest does not change the rules stated above regarding priority of a PMSI.

Choice "3" is incorrect. A judicial lien does not have priority over a properly perfected security interest in equipment collateral even if the PMSI was not perfected until after the lien attached, as long as the PMSI was perfected within 20 days after the debtor received possession of the equipment, which is the case here.

Topic D

QUESTION 1

Choice "2" is correct.

Section 11 of the Securities Act of 1933 permits lawsuits against the issuer and others for material misrepresentations or for omissions of material facts in the registration statement. Under Section 11, all the plaintiff needs to show is that the plaintiff acquired (not necessarily bought) the stock, the plaintiff suffered a loss, and there was a material misrepresentation or omission of a material fact. Thus, the plaintiff would have to prove that the plaintiff acquired the stock.

Choice "1" is incorrect. Privity is not a requirement of Section 11. Therefore, lack of privity is not a defense.

Choice "3" is incorrect because there is no requirement that the plaintiff prove negligence on the part of the issuer.

Choice "4" is incorrect because there is no requirement to prove fraud. Specifically, scienter and reliance (two elements of fraud) need not be proven by the plaintiff under Section 11.

QUESTION 2   MCQ-09574

Choice "2" is correct.

Registration is required under the Securities Exchange Act of 1934 in two cases: (1) if the securities are sold on a national exchange; or (2) if the issuer has at least 500 shareholders who are not accredited in any outstanding class and more than $10 million in assets. Because Price has 525 shareholders in its only class of stock, 520 of whom are unaccredited, and more than $10 million in assets, Price must file a registration statement.

Choice "1" is incorrect. It is not the number of shares that is causing Price to register, but rather the fact that it has 500 or more shareholders and more than $10 million in assets.

Choices "3" and "4" are incorrect because Price is required to register.

Topic E

QUESTION 1   MCQ-09103

Choice "3" is correct.

A partner can impose contract liability on the partnership and fellow partners when acting with apparent authority. It would be reasonable for a third party to believe that a partner could renew an existing lease.

Choice "1" is incorrect. Apparent authority depends on how things appear to third parties. It does not depend on a written partnership agreement.

Choice "2" is incorrect. A person is liable for his own torts and can be sued for them, regardless of whether the torts were committed on behalf of some business entity.

Choice "4" is incorrect because a partner has no apparent authority to admit liability in a lawsuit.

QUESTION 2   MCQ-09143

Choice "3" is correct.

A withdrawing partner is personally liable to creditors of the old partnership even if there is a hold harmless agreement. Fein was a partner in ABC. Thus, Fein is liable to the creditors of ABC. A hold harmless agreement allows Fein to recover from other partners any amounts he is required to pay to creditors.

Choices "1" and "2" are incorrect. A hold harmless agreement does not prevent creditors from holding an outgoing partner liable.

Choice "4" is incorrect. A hold harmless agreement allows Fein to recover from other partners any amounts he is required to pay to creditors. It is not limited to the amounts he has paid in excess of his proportionate share.

Regulation II

QUESTION 3 MCQ-09153

Choice "3" is correct.

A general partner may be a limited partner in the same partnership at the same time.

Choice "1" is incorrect. To form a limited partnership, there must be at least one general partner and one limited partner. General partners have unlimited liability.

Choice "2" is incorrect. Changes in limited partners do not cause dissolution.

Choice "4" is incorrect. The assignee does not become a substituted partner without the unanimous consent of all general and limited partners.

QUESTION 4 MCQ-09104

Choice "4" is correct.

Unless agreed otherwise, all LLC members have no liability beyond their investment. Thus, an LLC can be formed with limited liability for all members, unlike a limited partnership.

Choice "1" is incorrect. The articles of organization are filed with the state, not the operating agreement.

Choice "2" is incorrect. Unless otherwise agreed, an LLC is taxed like a partnership, not a corporation.

Choice "3" is incorrect. Virtually every state permits a one person LLC.

QUESTION 5 MCQ-09124

Choice "2" is correct.

The corporate entity may be disregarded and stockholders held personally liable for fraud, undercapitalization at the time of formation, or commingling of funds.

Choice "1" is incorrect because it is undercapitalization, not overcapitalization, that will permit piercing of the corporate veil.

Choice "3" is incorrect because a corporation may have more than one class of stock unless it is an S corporation.

Choice "4" is incorrect because the number of stockholders does not matter in determining whether a stockholder is personally liable.

Topic A

QUESTION 1

Choice "4" is correct.

There is no income tax on the value of inherited property. The gain on the sale is the difference between the sales price of $14,500 and Duffy's basis. Duffy's basis is the alternate valuation date elected by the executor. This is the value 6 months after date of death or date distributed if before 6 months. The property was distributed 4 months after death and the value that day ($14,500) is used for the basis. $14,500 − $14,500 = 0.

Choice "1" is incorrect. There is no income tax on the value of inherited property.

Choice "2" is incorrect. This is the basis of the stock if the alternate date had not been used. Heirs are not taxed on inheritances. The income or loss results when inherited property is sold.

Choice "3" is incorrect. There is no income tax on the value of inherited property. The gain on the sale is the difference between the sales price of $14,500 and Duffy's basis. Duffy's basis is the alternate valuation elected by the executor.

QUESTION 2

Choice "1" is correct.

Alice has a realized gain of $5,000 on the transaction: $25,000 sales price less $20,000 purchase price. However, she can reduce the gain, but not below zero, by the amount of loss her father could not deduct on the sale to her. Thus, Alice can reduce her gain by up to $10,000, but not below zero. Here, the gain is $5,000, so it is reduced to zero. Conner should have sold the stock in the open market so that he could deduct the entire loss. Alice could then have purchased the stock in the open market.

Choice "2" is incorrect. $5,000 is Alice's realized gain on the sale. However, she can reduce the gain, but not below zero, by the amount of loss her father could not deduct on the sale to her. The holding period in related party transactions starts with the new owner's period of ownership; therefore, this would be a short-term transaction.

Choice "3" is incorrect. Alice has a realized gain of $5,000 on the sale. In addition, she can reduce the gain, but not below zero, by the amount of loss her father could not deduct on the sale to her. The holding period in related party transactions starts with the new owner's period of ownership; therefore, this would be a short-term transaction. The following as indicated in this option.

Choice "4" is incorrect. Alice has a realized gain of $5,000 on the sale. In addition, she can reduce the gain, but not below zero, by the amount of loss her father could not deduct on the sale to her. The holding period in related party transactions starts with the new owner's period of ownership; therefore, this would be a short-term transaction.

QUESTION 3

Choice "3" is correct.

Because the machine was held more than 12 months and was depreciated, it was a §1231 asset. However, because it was sold at a gain, and the gain was less than the depreciation taken of $34,800 ($49,000 cost − $14,200 adjusted basis), all of the gain of $30,800 ($45,000 selling price − $14,200 adjusted basis) is gain recaptured by §1245 and there is no amount of §1231 gain.

Regulation III

Topic B

QUESTION 1 MCQ-09639

Choice "3" is correct.

Equipment is personal property. When over 40% of depreciable property is placed in service in the last quarter of the year (as is the case here), the MACRS mid-quarter convention applies to personal property.

Choice "1" is incorrect. After the maximum amount of Section 179 depreciation (expense election) is taken, the remaining amount of property placed in service in the current year is depreciable using the regular tax depreciation rules. Because Sima has positive Schedule C income in the current year, the maximum allowable Section 179 expense election may be claimed. There is no carryforward of the excess amount of purchases over the Section 179 expense limit for the current year, as these may be depreciated under the regular tax rules.

Choice "2" is incorrect. The MACRS half-year convention generally applies to personal property (including equipment); however, in this case, it does not apply, as all current year property (clearly over 40% of the total) was purchased in the last quarter of the current year.

Choice "4" is incorrect. Equipment is personal property. Residential real property is depreciated using the straight-line, mid-month convention over 27.5 years.

Topic C

QUESTION 1 MCQ-09596

Choice "1" is correct.

The gross estate of the first spouse to die includes 50% of the value of all property owned by the couple, regardless of which spouse furnished the original consideration, as they are considered to have owned the property as joint tenants with right of survivorship.

Choice "2" is incorrect. The taxpayers are considered to have owned the property jointly (tenants by the entirety or joint tenants with right of survivorship). One half of the value of the property will be included in the gross estate of the first spouse to die.

Choice "3" is incorrect. When property is held by a married couple as joint tenancy with right of survivorship or tenancy by the entirety, the gross estate includes one half of the value of the jointly owned property. The marital deduction is taken after calculation of the gross estate.

Choice "4" is incorrect. No such general law exists.

QUESTION 2 MCQ-09502

Choice "3" is correct.

Payments for college books, supplies, and dormitory food on behalf of an individual unrelated to the donor requires filing a gift tax return. Only payment of tuition to a qualified educational institution receives an unlimited gift tax exclusion.

Choices "1" and "2" are incorrect. There is an unlimited exclusion for direct payments of tuition and medical expenses.

Choice "4" is incorrect. Campaign contributions are not considered a gift. They are nondeductible.

Topic A

QUESTION 1   MCQ-09739

Choice "1" is correct.

Bob can only file as single. Bob does not meet the criteria to file as head of household. The head of household filing status is available to unmarried taxpayers who maintain a household for more than half the year for an unmarried son or daughter (not required to be a dependent, but must live with the taxpayer), father or mother (must be a dependent but not required to live with the taxpayer), or other dependent relative (must live with the taxpayer). In this case, Bob's mother does not meet the criteria to be considered his dependent. Specifically, she fails the qualifying relative gross income test.

Choice "2" is incorrect. Bob's mother is not Bob's dependent. Therefore, he cannot file as head of household.

Choice "3" is incorrect. "Qualifying single" is not an actual filing status. The filing statuses are: single, head of household, married filing separately, qualifying widow(er), and married filing jointly.

Choice "4" is incorrect. "Supporting single" is not an actual filing status. The filing statuses are: single, head of household, married filing separately, qualifying widow(er), and married filing jointly.

QUESTION 2   MCQ-09545

Choice "2" is correct.

Jeff and Rhonda may claim a total of three (3) dependents on their joint income tax return.

- Max is a qualifying child. He is full-time student under the age of 24, lives at home when he is not away for temporary absence at school, and is supported more than 50 percent by Jeff and Rhonda. The gross income test does not apply. Max is a dependent.

- Jen is also a qualifying child. While she is not a full-time student, she is still under the age of 19, lives at home, and is supported over 50 percent by her parents. The gross income test does not apply. Jen is a dependent.

- Joanne is a qualifying relative. She receives all of her support from Jeff and Rhonda, makes less than the gross income threshold amount in taxable income (her Social Security would not be taxable in these circumstances), does not file a joint return, and is a relative. Joanne is a dependent.

Choices "1", "3", and "4" are incorrect, per the above explanation.

Regulation IV

Topic B

QUESTION 1 MCQ-09481

Choice "1" is correct.

Rules: Alimony payments must be in cash, required by a divorce decree and be "periodic payments." Child support is nontaxable. Lump sum property settlements are not taxable. Alimony received per a divorce or separation agreement executed on or before 12/31/18 is taxable to the recipient.

Total payments made by Kyle were $45,000. Of that, $20,000 represents the lump sum property settlement. The remainder, $25,000, must first be applied against child support. Child support for the year was $20,000; 10 months × $2,000 per month. $5,000 remains to be classified as alimony and is taxable to Kaylie for 2018 because the divorce agreement was executed on or before 12/31/18.

Choice "2" is incorrect. $20,000 is the amount of the property settlement or the child support, neither of which are taxable to Kaylie.

Choice "3" is incorrect. The child support payments must first be subtracted to arrive at the taxable portion that is characterized as alimony.

Choice "4" is incorrect. The lump sum property settlement and any amounts characterized as child support are not taxable to Kaylie.

QUESTION 2 MCQ-09450

Choice "3" is correct.

Amounts received as compensation for services ($6,000) are taxable. In addition, the amount of the scholarship not used for qualified expenditures is taxable ($1,500) for a total taxable amount of $7,500.

Rule: Scholarships and fellowships not used to pay for qualified expenditures (tuition, fees, books) are taxable income to the recipient.

Choice "1" is incorrect, as it ignores both items that are taxable.

Choice "2" is incorrect, as it does not consider the $1,500 of the scholarship not used for qualified expenditures.

Choice "4" is incorrect. Scholarships used to pay for qualified expenditures to a degree-seeking student are excludable from gross income. This answer identifies the total scholarship received and compensation for teaching as taxable.

Topic C

QUESTION 1   MCQ-09738

Choice "1" is correct.

The rental real estate rule is an exception to the passive activity loss rules. Taxpayers may deduct up to $25,000 of net rental passive losses if they actively participate or manage the rental property and own more than 10 percent of the activity. The $25,000 is reduced by 50 percent of the excess of AGI over $100,000 and eliminated when AGI exceeds $150,000.

Choice "2" is incorrect. The rental real estate exception allows taxpayers to deduct up to $25,000 of net rental passive losses against ordinary income if the taxpayer actively participates in the rental activity.

Choice "3" is incorrect. The rental real estate exception allows taxpayers to deduct up to $25,000 of net rental passive losses against ordinary income if the taxpayer actively participates in the rental activity.

Choice "4" is incorrect. The rental real estate exception allows taxpayers to deduct up to $25,000 of net rental passive losses against ordinary income if the taxpayer actively participates in the rental activity.

Topic D

QUESTION 1   MCQ-09451

Choice "1" is correct.

Alimony payments received on a pre-2019 divorce or separation agreement are taxable as income to the recipient. However, payments that are required to be paid, even if the payee dies, are *not* considered to be payments for the support (alimony) and are considered to be amounts owed to the payee as part of the divorce settlement.

QUESTION 2   MCQ-09482

Choice "3" is correct.

Medical expenses include physical therapy (professional medical services) and insurance premiums providing reimbursement for medical care. Prescription drugs are considered medical care. Insurance against loss of income is not payment for medical care and therefore is not deductible. Qualified medical expenses must be reduced by insurance reimbursement ($2,000 + $500 − $1,500 = $1,000).

Choice "1" is incorrect. Insurance against loss of income is not payment for medical care and therefore is not deductible.

Choice "2" is incorrect. Medical expenses include physical therapy (professional medical services) and insurance premiums providing reimbursement for medical care.

Choice "4" is incorrect. Medical expenses include physical therapy (professional medical services) and insurance premiums providing reimbursement for medical care.

Regulation IV

Topic E

QUESTION 1 MCQ-09578

Choice "3" is correct.

The child tax credit is the only one of the above credits that is considered "refundable," which means that the credit can reduce tax below zero and result in a refund.

Choices "1", "2", and "4" are incorrect. All of these credits may only reduce total tax to zero.

Topic F

QUESTION 1 MCQ-09530

Choice "2" is correct.

Alternative minimum taxable income is calculated by starting with taxable income as follows:

Taxable income	$82,000
Add:	
State and local income taxes	3,000
	$85,000

Note: State and local income taxes are deductible for regular tax purposes, but not allowed for AMT purposes. Home mortgage interest is deductible for both regular and AMT purposes. Home equity interest not used to buy or build the house is not deductible for regular tax purposes or AMT purposes. Therefore, only state and local income taxes need to be added to taxable income to arrive at alternative minimum taxable income.

Topic A

QUESTION 1   MCQ-09469

Choice "3" is correct.

The charitable contribution deduction is limited to 10% of taxable income before the dividends received deduction and the charitable contribution deduction. 10% ($410,000 + $20,000) = $43,000. There will be a $2,000 carryforward to Year 7.

Topic B

QUESTION 1   MCQ-09516

Choice "2" is correct.

As a general rule, the basis of property received by a corporation by a transferor/shareholder is the greater of the basis of the transferred asset in the hands of the transferor/shareholder, or the debt assumed by the corporation. Therefore, The Worthington Corp.'s basis in the building is the same as Gearty's basis immediately prior to its contribution to the corporation.

Choice "1" is incorrect. The Worthington Corp.'s basis in the building is computed separately from any debt that it assumes related to the building.

Choice "3" is incorrect. The Worthington Corp. uses Gearty's basis, not the building's fair market value, as its basis. Furthermore, the debt assumed by The Worthington Corp. does not affect the basis of the building to The Worthington Corp.

Choice "4" is incorrect. The Worthington Corp. uses Gearty's basis, not the building's fair market value, as its basis.

QUESTION 2   MCQ-09484

Choice "3" is correct.

Income before special deductions includes sales, dividends received and cost of sales. It excludes the dividends received deduction, which is a "special" deduction.

Sales	$500,000
Cost of sales	(250,000)
Gross profit	250,000
Dividends received	25,000
Income before special deductions	$275,000

Choice "1" is incorrect. Cost of sales must be deducted.

Choice "2" is incorrect. Cost of sales must be deducted and 100%, not 80%, of the dividends received must be included in income before special deductions.

Choice "4" is incorrect. The $25,000 dividend must be included in income before special deduction.

                 Regulation Final Review

Regulation V

QUESTION 3

MCQ-09632

Choice "3" is correct.

Dividends are distributions of a corporation's earnings and profits, including accumulated (prior year) and current year E&P. Because the corporation had both accumulated E&P of $35,000 and current E&P of $15,000, the total amount of distributions classified as dividends is $50,000.

Choice "1" is incorrect. If a corporation has accumulated E&P and/or current year E&P, the distribution (depending upon amount) should be taxable as a dividend.

Choice "2" is incorrect. The amount taxable as a dividend is total E&P, not just the accumulated E&P.

Choice "4" is incorrect. The total distributions exceeds E&P. The excess will be treated as a return of basis and any remaining excess will be capital gain.

QUESTION 4

MCQ-09619

Choice "2" is correct.

$22,000 gain.

Rule: A corporation generally must recognize gain when it distributes appreciated property to its shareholders in any ordinary, nonliquidating distribution to the extent that the fair market value of the property exceeds its adjusted basis.

Fair market value per share	$ 20
Basis per share	(9)
Appreciation in value per share	$ 11
Number of shares distributed	× 2,000
Recognized gain	$22,000

Choices "1", "3", and "4" are incorrect, per the above rule.

QUESTION 5

MCQ-09500

Choice "2" is correct.

$50,000 capital gain. Property distributed in a complete liquidation of a corporation will be deemed to have been sold by the corporation at its fair market value and any gain or loss will be recognized by the liquidating corporation as a capital gain or loss.

Fair market value	$ 150,000
Basis	(100,000)
Gain	$ 50,000

The assets distributed are capital assets as opposed to business assets; therefore, the gain is a capital gain.

Topic C

QUESTION 1

Choice "2" is correct.

Rule: In order to be effective for the current taxable year, the S corporation election must be made by the 15th day of the third month of the taxable year. If the election is made after that date, it becomes effective on the first day of the next taxable year, January 1, Year 5, in this case.

QUESTION 2

Choice "2" is correct.

Rule: If ownership interests of an S corporation change within the taxable year, the income and/or loss to be allocated among the various shareholders will be made on a "per share, per day" basis.

S corporation loss for the year:

$36,500 / 365 days =	$ 100 (per day)
Number of days Duffy was a shareholder	40
Loss allocated to 40 days	$4,000
Duffy's ownership interest	50%
Loss allocated to Duffy for the year	$2,000

QUESTION 3

Choice "3" is correct.

S corporation status can be revoked if shareholders owning more than 50% of the total number of issued and outstanding shares consent. The specific percentage of voting and nonvoting shareholders is not considered, just the total. Holders of more than 25,000 total shares must approve the revocation.

Choices "1", "2", and "4" are incorrect. S corporation status can be revoked if shareholders owning more than 50% of the total number of issued and outstanding shares consent. The specific percentage of voting and nonvoting shareholders is not considered, just the total.

Regulation V

Topic D

QUESTION 1

Choice "1" is correct.

A partner's basis in a partnership is increased by the partner's share of partnership ordinary income, separately stated income, and tax-exempt income. $5,000 + 50\% \times (\$20,000 + \$8,000 + \$4,000) = \$21,000$.

Choice "2" is incorrect. Gray's basis is increased by $16,000, but the question asks what his total basis is on 12/31/Y4.

Choice "3" is incorrect. Gray's basis is increased by 50% of $20,000 + $4,000, or $12,000, but it is also increased by 50% of tax exempt income. This increase is added to the beginning basis.

Choice "4" is incorrect. Gray's basis is increased by 50% of ordinary income, or $10,000, but it is also increased by tax exempt and portfolio income. This increase is added to the beginning basis.

QUESTION 2

Choice "4" is correct.

Stacey will report 25% of the ordinary business income of $200,000 ($300,000 − $100,000), or $50,000, as income from partnerships on her tax return for the current year. The guaranteed payment is an allowable deduction for the partnership against ordinary income. Stacey will also report 25% of the interest income $2,500 on her Schedule B and 25% of the charitable contributions $4,000 on her Schedule A for the current year.

Choice "1" is incorrect. These are the amounts that will be reported for the partnership as a whole on Schedule K. The partnership will also report the detailed business revenues and expenses (including 100% of the guaranteed payment) on its Form 1065.

Choice "2" is incorrect. This answer shows the amounts that Nick would report on his tax return for the current year. The ordinary income would include $50,000 of income from partnerships and $30,000 ordinary income from the guaranteed payment (likely also subject to self-employment tax).

Choice "3" is incorrect. This answer assumes that the guaranteed payment is not an allowable expense of the partnership (or Stacey) and adds it back to the net ordinary business income of the partnership. ($300,000 − $100,000 + $30,000 = $230,000; $230,000 / 4 = $57,500.) The other columns are correct. Stacey will also report 25% of the interest income $2,500 on her Schedule B and 25% of the charitable contributions $4,000 on her Schedule A for the current year.

QUESTION 3

Choice "2" is correct.

In a nonliquidating distribution, the partner takes the partnership basis for assets distributed. This basis cannot exceed the partner's basis in the partnership.

Choice "1" is incorrect. This is Day's remaining basis in the partnership, not the basis for the land.

Choices "3" and "4" are incorrect. In a nonliquidating distribution, the partner takes the partnership basis for assets distributed.

QUESTION 4

Choice "4" is correct.

When Fox sells his partnership interest, capital gain or loss on the sale is recognized. To the extent that there are Sec. 751(a) hot assets (unrealized receivables or substantially appreciated inventory), the partner must recognize ordinary income or loss. In this case, the partnership has no Sec. 751 assets. The amount realized less the partner's basis in the partnership is the capital gain or loss. The amount realized is $75,000 ($50,000 cash received + $25,000 relief of debt). The partner's basis in the partnership is $60,000. Thus, the capital gain is $75,000 − $60,000, or $15,000.

Choice "1" is incorrect. Since there are no Sec. 751 assets, the gain or loss must be capital, not ordinary.

Choice "2" is incorrect. Since there are no Sec. 751 assets, the gain or loss must be capital, not ordinary.

Choice "3" is incorrect. The amount realized must include the $25,000 debt relief.

Topic E

QUESTION 1

Choice "1" is correct.

DNI is gross income minus expenses with certain modifications, as follows:

Taxable interest	$20,000
Long-term capital gains	10,000
Gross income	30,000
Less: Administrative expenses	(5,000)
Less: Modification for capital gains	(10,000)
DNI	$15,000

Choice "2" is incorrect. The administrative expenses reduce the DNI.

Choice "3" is incorrect. Net long-term capital gains allocable to corpus is not included in DNI. The administrative expenses reduce the DNI.

Choice "4" is incorrect. Net long-term capital gains allocable to corpus is not included in DNI.

QUESTION 2

Choice "2" is correct.

Rule: The income tax return of a trust on Form 1041 is due on the 15th day of the fourth month after the close of its taxable year.

Lyon's current year return would be due on April 15 of the following year. If that were a Saturday or Sunday or a legal holiday, the return is not due until the next day that is not a Saturday or Sunday or a legal holiday.

Regulation V

Topic F

QUESTION 1 MCQ-09657

Choice "4" is correct.

Although an organization may have tax-exempt status, it may become subject to regular corporate income tax on income from a business enterprise that is not related to its tax exempt purpose (UBI). There is a $1,000 specific deduction from such income, and certain other income is excluded from taxation as UBI. Income from the research of a college or hospital is one of the types of income that is specifically excluded.

Choice "1" is incorrect. Unrelated business income does not include any activity where all of the work is performed by unpaid workers (volunteers); thus, the fact that the organization uses unpaid workers makes the business or activity "related" and not taxable.

Choice "2" is incorrect. The fact that the activity results in a loss does not exclude that activity from the definition of an unrelated business. If expenses exceed income, a net operating loss exists, which is subject to carryback and carryover provisions of net operating losses.

Choice "3" is incorrect. Unrelated business income is not 100% taxable on the organization's tax return. There is a $1,000 specific deduction from such income, and certain other income is excluded from taxation as UBI.

QUESTION 2 MCQ-09658

Choice "3" is correct.

This is a false statement. An organization operated primarily for the purpose of carrying in a trade or business for profit cannot claim tax exemption on the grounds that all of its profits are payable to exempt organizations (e.g., a "feeder organization"). It must rely on its own activities and exempt nature to gain tax exemption.

Choice "1" is incorrect. This is a correct statement.

Choice "2" is incorrect. This is a correct statement. For organizations that normally have less than $50,000 in annual gross receipts, a 990-N ("electronic postcard") is filed with the IRS to provide the following information: (1) the tax identification number of the organization; (2) the tax year of the organization; (3) the legal name, physical address, and Internet address (if applicable) of the organization; (4) the name and address of the principal officer of the organization; and (5) a statement that the annual gross receipts of the organization regularly do not exceed the $50,000 limit.

Choice "4" is incorrect. This is a correct statement.